RENT BOY

RENT

BOY

**How One Man Spent
20 Years Falling Off
the Property Ladder**

PETE MAY

MAINSTREAM
PUBLISHING

EDINBURGH AND LONDON

First published in Great Britain in 2004 by
MAINSTREAM PUBLISHING COMPANY (EDINBURGH) LTD
7 Albany Street
Edinburgh EH1 3UG

ISBN 1 84018 857 X

A catalogue record for this book is available from the British Library

Typeset in Comic Sans, Stone Informal and UniversBK

Printed in Great Britain by
Antony Rowe, Chippenham, Wiltshire

For Nicola, Lola and Nell

CONTENTS

Acknowledgements

A big thank you to Bill Campbell at Mainstream for commissioning this book – even if he did think it was about my secret life in the sex industry. Also to Deborah Warner for her painstaking fact-checking and editing; her new-found knowledge of 1980s trivia will surely make her a must for every pub quiz team.

My partner Nicola deserves special praise for tolerating several months of being a property widow during the writing of this book. Thank you too to Phill Jupitus, Joe Norris and Nick Toms, and any editors who have ever commissioned my rants about property, including Bill Williamson at *Midweek* who published the original 'Why I'm Still a Rent Boy' feature.

The Council of Mortgage Lenders, Shelter, *The London Encyclopaedia*, the *Chronicle of the 20th Century* and numerous other sources have all provided valuable help with research.

Thanks also to everyone I've ever rented from or flat-shared with – without you, I wouldn't be where I am today.

Preface

Man rents flat. Man gets evicted. Man fails to climb on property ladder. Again. It's not necessarily the stuff of Hollywood movies, but it's been the story of my life and plenty of other people's too.

Britain is a nation obsessed by property. A glance through the TV schedules reveals numerous programmes detailing our love of buying, selling and making over properties. The likes of *Location, Location, Location, I Want That House, Trading Up, Hot Property, Up Your Street, Escape To The Country, Des Res, Building the Dream, House Invaders, Safe As Houses, House Doctor, Ground Force* and *Changing Rooms* all highlight our love of bricks and mortar.

Yet I have spent more than 20 years floundering beneath the bottom rung of the property ladder. I was the prospective first-time buyer who was always on the verge of being priced out of the capital. Talk to anyone who has moved to London and hopefully they will identify with my tales of endless queues for rooms advertised in the *Standard* followed by nightmare flatmates.

Since arriving in London in 1981, most of my efforts have been devoted to securing an affordable, permanent place to live. Back then Mrs Thatcher was creating a 'property-owning democracy' – council houses were being sold off and property prices were starting to increase, along with the number of homeless people. People and money were being attracted to the south-east of England and London had the most inflated property market in the UK. The word 'home' had previously referred to a place to live. Now a home was an investment opportunity.

Throughout the 1980s, everyone I met told me to get on the property ladder before it was too late. They shut up for a time during the property slump of the early 1990s, but then it started all over again. Sometimes I'd think that if only it were possible to find permanent, affordable rented housing in London, I wouldn't care about buying. But it wasn't. After years of battling notices to quit, asbestos in my walls, withheld deposits and numerous arguments over house rotas, buying a property came to seem like my only avenue of escape.

My career as a freelance journalist and writer was always beset by the underlying fear that I was committing property suicide and would never be able to buy a home. At times, I felt like a modern-day heretic.

Today, our society is more unequal than ever: there are two nations in the country, the property owners and the renting classes. If you're a potential first-time buyer in London, you can't afford even the most meagre of properties without the aid of inherited wealth or rich parents. Figures from Shelter reveal that while the price of a loaf of bread has risen sixfold since 1960, the cost of the average house is 60 times more expensive. Should it really be so hard to find a roof above your head?

But this book is more than an extended tale of years of property market madness. It's also a tour throughout numerous regions of London, the city I have come to love. The vagaries of the rental market have seen me pacing the paving stones of Turnpike Lane, West Kensington, Hammersmith, Parsons Green, Fulham Broadway, Camberwell, Neasden, Westbourne Park, Victoria, Elephant and Castle, Highbury and Finsbury Park. My best friend for the last 23 years has been the London A–Z.

While writing this book, what's been striking is how accommodation has affected nearly every aspect of my life: the friends I've made, the people I've fought, every woman I've dated, every job I've applied for or been sacked from.

In some chapters, the names of both the innocent and guilty have been changed, but everything else is true.

PREFACE

Above all, I hope you'll find some of my stories amusing. Maybe you'll come and join me: 'Author has large spacious book to let, close to all amenities, no references required, viewing on request.' Welcome to my life as a rent boy.

Pete May
May 2004

1. All Stations to Cockfosters

Westbury Avenue, Turnpike Lane, London N22
November 1981 to June 1982

Turnpike Lane was my passport to the metropolis of London. Just like the sleeve notes said on the first Dexys Midnight Runners album, *Searching for the Young Soul Rebels*, I had been 'lying low waiting for the big one'. Lying very low. In my home town of Brentwood. But now this 22-year-old young soul rebel was departing from post-student Essex ennui.

After nine months on the dole in Brentwood, I was escaping to the bright light of a main artery road off Turnpike Lane, London. Like Jude the Obscure gazing at the elusive spires of Oxford University, I would wonder at the dreaming spires of Wood Green shopping centre – only for me, they were attainable. Jude, mate, you should have used the flat-share columns in *City Limits*. Or maybe even *Loot*.

As several of my friends frequently pointed out, Bored Town was an anagram of Brentwood. It had hippies, commuters and Conservative voters, and no tower blocks. Visiting the town today, it actually seems quite a pleasant place to live. Back then, though, like every young punk turned Dexys fan returning home after three years away at university, it seemed stifling.

I'd read George Orwell and studied the lyrics of 'Smithers-Jones' by The Jam. I had no desire to spend every working day commuting along the same stretch of railway track from a dormitory town to Liverpool Street.

Mrs Thatcher had been Prime Minister for two years. I believed in the mixed economy, Keynesian economics and social justice – she didn't. Thanks to the Government's monetarist policies, unemployment was just about to hit three million and there were few opportunities for English graduates with only an extensive knowledge of Costello, Weller, Rowland, Dickens, Hemingway and the romantic poets to offer on their CV. Nor did I have any real idea about what I wanted to do. Except that suits, commuting and being trapped in a job by a huge mortgage was never going to happen to me.

Seven days previously, I'd travelled up to London to see Dexys Midnight Runners' acclaimed *Projected Passion Revue* at the Old Vic theatre. For this young Dexys aficionado, it was an awesome event. The band wore boxing boots and sat in cafés. They drank tea. They refused to give interviews. Instead, they took out ads in the music papers and announced: 'We are not a band, we don't play gigs and we don't make albums. We're a group, we perform shows and we intend to make an LP.' Right.

Everything about Dexys' leader Kevin Rowland was intense, pure and precious, to borrow a few of his favourite soundbites. Dexys' pronouncements were preposterous and completely humourless, but calculated to appeal to unemployed and earnest English graduates like myself.

The reason Dexys could get away with all this was that their music was brilliant; that night, the horns playing the unforgettable intro of 'Tell Me When My Light Turns Green' really did reach out to everyone in the Old Vic. Rowland had seen quite a bit in his 23 years and so too had I in my 22. Although, back then, I had little idea that the following 22 years or so of nomadic nightmares were to create in me the sort of emotional intensity Kevin Rowland could only fantasise about.

That Dexys lyric on 'Tell Me When My Light Turns Green', mixing religious references with Rowland's desire to escape depression and losing and boozing, seemed to encapsulate much of my life. Although it wasn't spiritual salvation that I needed so much as a flat and a career. For several days after that concert I felt inspired and sensed that maybe my life would get better. A week later, it did. Pete May was to don his donkey jacket, escape suburban Essex and make it to Turnpike Lane.

Moving was not a new experience. Earlier in my life, I had learned that existence was just the continual shifting of the atoms that constitute the human form from one rented abode to another. At Lancaster University, I had spent two years in halls of residence and one year living off campus in Morecambe (a place so full of old-age pensioners it was dubbed 'the cemetery with lights').

My first attempt at independent living had lasted one week and one cacophonous party, then even the students decided the flat was falling down and fled; there had been a disastrous two-week period living with Fred and Ivy, a surrogate mum and dad. A lovely old couple – Fred sitting in front of the gas fire telling us that England's Bob Latchford was 'a puddin'' and Ivy serving our meals on time. But it wasn't the independent life a young student desired.

Then came a bedsit in the West End (of Morecambe, that is) with its warlike landlady Mrs Peace, who once interrupted a house party with the incredulous cry of 'Party! I call this an invasion!' and would often leave notes on my breadboard saying, 'This flat is filthy!' – which it probably was, but hey, I was a student.

After graduating, I had a vague intention of maybe taking what would now be referred to as a 'gap year' before perhaps going to teacher training college. My career planning was generally inept, but at least some options could be discarded – working for a bank in the City the summer before my university course started had soon convinced me that corporate life was about as exciting as the concept triple album *Tales From Topographic Oceans* by prog rockers Yes.

On graduating, my first job was in a bar in Morecambe during the summer season, serving drunken Glaswegians standing six deep demanding 'seven pints of lagger and a Groose, Jimmy'. One of them swore that I looked like a young James Mason and always called me 'James': about the only good thing to come out of the job. At the time, my home was a shared flat high up on the hill in Lancaster with fine views overlooking the city and the meandering

River Lune. Sadly, it was only let for the summer until the student occupiers returned for term-time.

Next came a temporary job as a shop assistant in a clearance shop for Burton and a move to a place nearer the centre of Lancaster. In the house were three students and Bob, a sad unemployed lorry driver who liked westerns on telly. A victim of the mass unemployment that was sweeping Britain under the new Conservative government, he reminded me of Stephen Blackpool in *Hard Times*.

The job with Burton finished once the stock had been sold off. Huge amounts of condensation gathered on the rotting windows in my bedroom as I mournfully played *Closer* by Joy Division, The Cure's 'Seventeen Seconds' and *Scary Monsters* by David Bowie. Jobs in Lancaster were rarer than people who had a conciliatory word to say for Margaret Thatcher and, feeling like a loser ex-student hanging around people who were still at university, I retreated back to Essex at the start of 1981.

My parents were tenant farmers on the edges of Brentwood. My childhood had been spent in a large five-bedroom farmhouse which was superficially grand but owned by the council. Today, we'd probably fall into the lower-middle-class category. My mum's family were working class made good from Stoke-on-Trent; her father was a clerk who became an officer in the First World War and then worked for British Rail selling freight for the rest of his life. My paternal grandfather had run an insurance company in Upminster. We had a lounge rather than a living room, ate tea rather than dinner. Nor was my dad a gentleman farmer: he worked hard, rarely took holidays and sat down to eat smelling of dung after long days with his cattle.

It wasn't a rural farming community at all. My dad's farm was the last bit of country before greater London. You could see the Post Office Tower on clearer summer nights and my influences were as much West Ham, Romford Market, Mister Byrite and The Faces as bucolic wanderings in bluebell-strewn woods.

My father believed in self-reliance – having built up his own farming business from nothing – and I had no problem with that.

ALL STATIONS TO COCKFOSTERS

There was no expectation that anyone would ever buy a house or set up a trust fund for me. Whatever I achieved in my life would be through my own efforts and savings. Maybe it was all a bit like that old Johnny Cash song, 'A Boy Named Sue'. My parents knew that by allowing me to negotiate my way through numerous accommodation nightmares, I would eventually be inspired to write books about my life as a rent boy.

What I did know was that I had to find somewhere to live on my own. My dad favoured three possible careers for me: farming, farming and farming. Apart from not liking working with animals, hating getting up early, not wanting to be subjected to military-style toughening-up techniques, not being practical and not wanting to spend the rest of my life living in the same house that I'd been brought up in, I was quite well suited to it.

My father's desire for me, his only son, to take over his tenancy was understandable and many farming fathers down the centuries will have felt the same way. No doubt I'll soon be insisting that my daughters loaf for several years before becoming financially challenged freelance hacks and moderately successful writers. But you can't make someone take up a profession they don't like. And for a 22-year-old punk disciple, farming was hardly a rock 'n' roll lifestyle (unless you were Roger Daltrey, that is). I wanted to have new experiences, to live in new places and although I had no real idea about career opportunities (apart from it being a record by The Clash), I knew that I wanted to write.

Living with my mum and dad was not an option for a few months anyway, as my dad was in complex negotiations with the council over their plans to route the M25 through his land. He hoped to secure compensation on the grounds that he would no longer be able to run a farm that was cut in two by a busy road. He believed his case would not be helped by an unemployed and able-bodied son living at home whom the council might erroneously think could run the place.

So there was a disastrous spell renting a bedsit in soulless Shenfield (which I quickly left) and then nine months sharing a decent house in suburban and sedate Rose Valley, Brentwood.

There, my flatmates were my old school friend Paul, his girlfriend Katie (both just graduated from the University of East Anglia), Kevin, a graduate in Russian working as a milkman, who loved Henry Miller, wanted to be a professional gambler and introduced me to the first Dexys album, and a phantom character we referred to as 'Motorway Man', an engineer working on the M25, whom none of us encountered, ever.

By the age of twenty-two, I had already lived in seven rented homes and two different halls of residence. Some of us are born to rent, some achieve renting status and others have tenancy agreements thrust upon us. When they come to put those blue plaques on all my former residences, they're going to have to make a lot of them.

Joining a temporary employment agency had at last given me hope of leaving Brentwood. Paul and Katie, my flatmates from Rose Valley, had found work through the same agency and moved into a shared council flat in Lisson Grove, Paddington. Now the agency had come up with a position for me at the Housing Corporation, situated at the top of Tottenham Court Road, opposite Warren Street Tube station.

My job involved sifting through huge, teetering piles of mainly indecipherable HAR 10/2 forms (with statistical appendix). These forms had been sent out to every housing association in the country and were a bizarre mass of boxes, arrows and formulae; they looked as if they had been designed by Professor Stephen Hawking. They were so complex that no one could possibly fill them in correctly without a knowledge of particle and string theory. It was my task to fill in the missing boxes and if necessary ring up the relevant housing association to confirm the correct figures for their new-build schemes.

At the other end of the offices was a statistician called Graham. He had a beard (no one had a beard in 1981) and he liked both Yes and Margaret Thatcher, which was, to my mind, utterly inexplicable in a seemingly decent human being. I would pass the completed forms on to Graham. He would then pass them on to his cricket-loving boss Eric, who sat in an enclosed office to our left. This work made Sir Geoffrey Howe's speeches on money supply sound interesting. The biggest excitement was the arrival of the tea lady twice a day. Never has a clock's second hand moved as slowly as the one on that office wall.

But that job was my key to moving to London. Nobody would consider letting to the UB40 generation. My tenure at the Housing Corporation seemed to expand even quicker than my piles of HAR 10/2 forms. The forms were going to take aeons to process and, armed with a semi-permanent job, I was finally able to answer flat-share ads.

The renting section of the right-on listings mag *City Limits* seemed a likely option, as anyone who advertised in it would hopefully be both radical and tolerant of an ex-student with no proper job. *City Limits* was the product of a collective run by former staff from *Time Out* who had quit when the principle of equal wages for all was abandoned. It listed exciting events in London, such as alternative cabaret, and carried endless articles on Hackney Council and dodgy Stoke Newington police officers. It was read by ex-students, social workers and women with dangly earrings who wore leather jackets.

For the first and only time in my London flat-sharing life, I got the first flat I applied for. Alan, a bearded 34-year-old sociology lecturer in Turnpike Lane, was looking for a 'non-smoker to rent own room'. Alan was both an unreconstructed hippy and a sociologist, so facial hair was no doubt a part of his job description.

His flat was on the ground floor of a house in Westbury Avenue. Turnpike Lane Tube was on the Piccadilly Line and only nine stops from Covent Garden. The station itself, with its high entrance hall and curved facades, was a rather fine example of '30s-style municipal architecture. Westbury Avenue was a busy main road linking Green Lanes and Wood Green High Road with Lordship Lane. Near the house was a pub called the Westbury which was full of blokes in paint-spattered sweatshirts drinking lager; several years later, I would recognise them as the prototype for Harry Enfield's character Loadsamoney.

RENT BOY

The houses in Westbury Avenue and most of the backstreets up to Wood Green were more or less identical late-Victorian and early-twentieth-century red-brick constructions with white bay windows, reeking of the aspirational lower-middle classes. The sort of places Chas and Dave might have been brought up in saying 'Gertcha!' before going up the old Spurs.

Alan's front door was a solid blue, with green tiling around the porch and a small enclave at the front of the house containing the dustbins and a few sparse bushes. There was a front room, a long corridor leading to Alan's room, the bathroom, what was to be my room and a kitchen at the back of the flat. It would do; anything to escape Brentwood.

Within days, my dad gave me a lift with my stuff, travelling along the North Circular and onto Westbury Avenue. It seems incredible now, when moving requires a team of three men working for two days and costing nearly two grand, that all my possessions fitted in the back of my dad's minivan. There was my new hi-fi, with huge round knobs on the front of the amp, a cassette deck and lots of flashing lights. A battered manual typewriter, several boxes of books, a case full of clothes and a box of tapes made up the rest of my possessions.

Despite his great age and hippy beard, Alan appeared to be a decent bloke. At university, it had seemed the world was divided neatly between young people like me, who listened to punk or rock music, and old people like my parents, who listened to Beethoven and Engelbert Humperdinck. But Alan could converse about Bob Dylan and make lengthy critiques of Maggie Thatcher. Best of all, he had a hugely attractive girlfriend called Bronwyn, who was a fellow sociology lecturer with red hennaed hair and dangly earrings.

Alan and Bronwyn were unfailingly social to their post-punk lodger. Sometimes we'd all take the bus up the hill to a trendy pub in the more middle-class environs of Hornsey, a place that seemed to be populated by a collective of *City Limits*-reading social workers and lecturers. Over our pints, we bemoaned the demise of Keynesian economics and reasoned that with three million unemployed, anti-nuclear demonstrations all over Europe and our persuasive coalition of sociology lecturers and itinerant ex-students, Thatcher would soon be gone forever.

Already London was helping me learn valuable lessons in life: really old people in their 30s could be interesting and they even led active sex lives despite their addiction to listening to Bob Dylan singing 'Desolation Row' in the sitting room and frequent discussions of one-dimensional man Herbert Marcuse, whoever he played for.

One of Alan's big selling points for the area was that there was an alternative bookshop at Wood Green. It could be reached through a maze of backstreets from Alan's house and in those pre-Internet, indeed pre-computer days it was the only place you could easily find radical reading material such as *Spare Rib*, *Socialist Worker* and *Militant*. Its few customers all looked like Alan and Bronwyn and were apparently unaware that the rest of Wood Green was too busy buying cheap lager at Safeway to have the time to pick up a copy of *Marxists in Literature* or *Class War*.

Most of my life was spent away from Turnpike Lane. Like Paul Weller, I was going underground. On my first night in Alan's flat, I went out with Paul and Katie and their friend Helen to see *The French Lieutenant's Woman* starring Meryl Streep and Jeremy Irons. This was the London of high art I had been seeking. Here you could see a different film *every night of the week*.

The very act of travelling on the Piccadilly Line seemed a uniquely exciting activity. On the Tube each morning, there were women in ra-ra skirts with fluffed-up hair who looked like members of Bananarama. After changing at King's Cross onto the Victoria Line and travelling to Warren Street, my hours of form shuffling at the Housing Corporation would begin. Then drinks after work in pubs off Oxford Street or maybe something more unusual. Paul and Katie had discovered cocktail bars where New Romantic men wore waist-length, tight-fitting jackets and improbably flouncy cuffs. Paul and Katie's flatmate Brian was exceedingly camp and spoke with a pronounced Birmingham accent. He also wore make-up and worshipped David Sylvian of

Japan. Brummie blokes in sky blue bum-hugging suits? London was a new and exotic place indeed.

In the spring of 1982, my mornings began with the Human League's 'Don't You Want Me' on my radio alarm, followed by news of Argentina's invasion of the Falkland Islands. Alan and I both agreed that Margaret Thatcher's plans to counter this invasion with a Task Force were absolute folly and that it would all end in electoral disaster.

While Britain drifted towards war, Paul and Katie discovered a party in Stoke Newington's Church Street. There was much raucous dancing to The Beatles' 'Twist and Shout' and I found myself entwined with an art therapist who was a fanatical fan of right-on feminist outfit the Au Pairs. She even had dangly earrings. Having extracted her phone number, I walked down Green Lanes all the way to Westbury Avenue, as the light emerged and the birds twittered drunkenly at dawn. It felt like being Tom Waits. A week later, the art therapist even went on a date with me, although I was soon to learn that women who wanted steady relationships were rarer in London than decent rented accommodation.

By mid-1982, it was clear to me that living with someone who owned the house was not what I wanted. Although I did my best to put the rubbish out and wash up, when Alan started complaining about not drying the dishes properly before putting them away, I knew that it was time to move on. Living with your landlord, you were always conscious that it was his property, not yours. There were no big arguments, though, and he understood my reasons for wanting to move somewhere more central.

Now I had a Doctor Marten shoe-hold on the capital, it was time to find somewhere more attractive to young people my age. Flat-sharing was my best hope of cracking London.

A Task Force was heading back from the Falklands as Margaret Thatcher announced 'Rejoice!' – my own task was simply to find a flat-share with interesting people, seduce one of those women in ra-ra skirts on the Tube and become the next Henry Miller. My endless sojourn around the postcodes of London had begun.

ALL STATIONS TO COCKFOSTERS

MORTGAGE PROSPECTS: The applicant has no permanent job, no deposit and no desire to join the wage slaves at the age of 22. He states that he does not intend to grow up, calm down or end up working for the clampdown and seems to have no suitable skills for the current labour market. Next!

AVERAGE HOUSE PRICE IN GREATER LONDON: £36,594

2. The Young Ones

Comeragh Road, West Kensington, London W14
June 1982 to November 1982

Comeragh Road was perfect. At last, I was moving into a shared flat in a trendy part of London with four other young people. After answering an ad in the *Evening Standard* for a room in West Kensington, I was interviewed by Sean. He was a thin, intellectual-looking character wearing round, steel-rimmed glasses with black tinted lenses. He had an Iggy Pop poster on his bedroom wall. Encouragingly, Sean was on the dole and wasn't at all worried by the fact that my employment at the Housing Corporation was temporary and in fact about to expire altogether. Nor was he rejoicing at victory in the Falklands like some of the other potential flatmates who had interviewed me.

Sean was planning to relax all summer before going to university the next year. He was a huge admirer of the Stranglers and a keen reader of black-spined Penguin Classics. In what must have rated as one of the most unusual flat-share interviews of all time, he recommended Maupassant as much better than Thomas Hardy before signing me up.

The other pivotal person in the household was Julia, a busy graduate who was working for an American law firm. A born self-improver and one-woman encyclopedia of evening classes, she could easily recite educational opportunities from the plethora advertised in the Floodlight catalogue, the capital's guide to adult education. Unlike Sean and myself, she was the most organised person on the planet and we had to book time in her diary just to speak to her about the washing up. Invariably, she would preface her sentences with cries of 'I'm very happy', before complaining 'No one's done the washing up!' There was a certain mutual fascination between Sean and Julia, though. She had discovered Covent Garden and Sean and myself spent many an afternoon carrying her shopping bags home, a little like K.'s assistants in Kafka's *The Castle*, we thought.

Sean and Julia had interlocking rooms, which meant that Sean could only get to his room by first walking through Julia's. Landlords seem to specialise in converting rooms into spaces that offer their tenants no privacy. Eventually, their lives were to interlock again, some seven or eight years later, when they finally started going out with each other and ultimately married. It was a bit like an early, British version of *Friends*. How many other couples in Britain must have been brought together through the vagaries of dodgy partition walls?

The remaining flatmates came in a twosome: Diane and Jane, vertical-haired Goths from Leeds. Diane's barnet was peroxide blonde, Jane's beetroot red. Their day jobs were relatively mundane, but their evenings were spent in pursuit of pink-haired hedonism: numerous pints of snakebite or other stimulants in various pubs and clubs, while seducing boys with their Goth spells.

One of their favourite haunts was the Moscow Arms in Notting Hill. Everyone looked as spiky and peroxided as them in there and someone like me felt incredibly straight for simply experimenting on my hair with a hint of black henna (which had since taken on a slightly purple hue).

The District Line Tube emerged from the darkness of Earls Court and suddenly you were overground and seemingly out of London. Just walking to the house from West Kensington station in the June sunlight was an exquisite pleasure. Armed with a new A–Z, I revelled in the freedom and possibilities of London.

Comeragh Road began with a number of elegant four-storey houses, with refined white balconies and roof terraces. The people who lived there had probably never even heard of Turnpike Lane, let alone been there. It was a wide street, covering four lanes, revealing an unusual amount of blue sky for London. Halfway along, the white houses gave way to red-brick Victorian properties. They were slightly blackened by a century of exposure to industry and the motors of the Talgarth Road, and reminded me a little of the smoke-encrusted homes around my grandparents' house in Stoke-on-Trent.

This end of the road had a pleasing air of genteel poverty and our house was more neglected than most. The woodwork in the windows did not look solid and was covered in peeling white paint. The black-painted front door of our house was ancient. There were white wooden fences around the balconies on the first and second floors which looked decidedly dangerous should anyone choose to lean on them.

Our landlord was a shadowy man called Mr Draper. Leonard Rossiter had created an enduring landlord stereotype in his classic role as Rigsby in *Rising Damp* and it was surprising how many landlords still conformed to this stereotype. Perhaps it was something they were taught when they did their Higher National Diplomas in advanced dodgy-sofa-buying for property owners.

During his rent-collecting forays, Mr Draper exuded a timid, whispering insincerity. We were on a six-month holiday let and hoped to renegotiate at the end of our current deal. You couldn't really imagine any sane person wanting to holiday with us, the infamous five: two Goths, two loafers and one evening-class expert. Holiday lets were actually a device used by landlords to ensure you had no tenancy rights and could be easily evicted at the end of the let.

That summer was a happy period. Comeragh Road was a homely place, even if the furniture looked as if it hadn't been changed for a decade or three. But the battered old maroon sofa was comfortable and the ancient TV just about good enough for watching World Cup games. My room was in need of some 'renovation', as the estate agents would have said, but it was also huge. As an excellent and irrepressibly catchy single from Dexys

Midnight Runners called 'Come On Eileen' played on my new JVC turntable, I could clumsily bounce around doing my Kevin Rowland impersonation while psyching myself up for parties. The artwork of that single, with Kevin and the 'Dexys babe' in dungarees walking arm in arm, seemed to sum up the optimism of the summer. In fact, Julia feared that I really would hum that song forever as the 45 was played for the 20th time. Toora loo rye aye, indeed.

West Kensington was proving a great location. It was close to two tubes, West Kensington and Barons Court, yet on the quiet roads you had no idea that London's busiest traffic artery, Talgarth Road, was a couple of streets away. There was even The Queen's Tennis Club near Barons Court, to add to the village sensation. Not that the officials outside would ever have allowed someone like me in there.

By West Kensington Tube, there was a spacious pub called the Three Kings with a bustling clientele of young people, making it an ideal pre-party boozer. The ever-convivial Diane and Jane made friends with the Aussies in the Barons Court Tavern in Comeragh Road. Hammersmith was a ten-minute walk or single Tube stop away for drinks and concerts. Across Talgarth Road it was a short walk up North End Road to Kensington High Street where Katie was now working for an investment bank. We'd frequently meet in Kensington High Street for drinks after work, or move on to the Lyric bar at Hammersmith, or a variety of pubs around Notting Hill Gate.

There was a kebab shop and a chippy in the North End Road for those moments when none of us dared enter our kitchen. Even the flies were reluctant to land there sometimes. Teetering mounds of plates, grease congealing with festering tomato puree as spaghetti bolognese mutated into a new and more dangerous entity, Sean's dog-ends in mugs of half-drunk tea, a cooker that threatened to ignite the house with one twist of a loose knob – sometimes takeaways were the only hope of self-preservation.

My work at the Housing Corporation soon ended and I returned to the ranks of the three million unemployed. Those huge piles of HAR 10/2 forms (with statistical appendix) finally ran out and the statisticians began to design even more incomprehensible documents to baffle the housing associations with the following year. There was the distant hope of a place at teacher training college, but really all I knew was that I never wanted to work with a HAR 10/2 form again.

My job had enabled me to save a little money, but not enough to disqualify me from receiving benefits. As for my rent, it would now be paid for by the department of social security. Sean and I took to a life of intellectual loafing. We'd discuss Maupassant and Flaubert while taking in some afternoon and evening World Cup matches. Or I'd joke that Sean was going through his 'Bazarov the Nihilist' phase in a knowing reference to Turgenev.

Does a man really need to work when he can sit for hours by a ghetto-blaster listening to the Stranglers' 'Hanging Around', just waiting for Jean Jacques Burnel's bass to come in? After listening to the group's 'Don't Bring Harry', we had picked up on the line, 'He is a beast of luxury', and decided that we were going to be beasts of luxury, too. Sometimes we'd open the windows and sit on the old balcony looking over Comeragh Road, being careful not to lean on the rickety white wooden railings, remarking how we should sip cocktails in the mornings as we watched the people below go to work.

In August, we decided to have a house party and invited everyone any of us knew. If you were there, you probably won't remember it, nor can I beyond 'Come On Eileen' playing at full volume and Julia doing her Kevin Rowland, arms-above-the-head dance; Diane and Jane being surrounded by people with equally silly haircuts; every room and the stairs being full of a multitude of bodies; the art therapist I got off with at a party in Stoke Newington turning up and getting a lift home with someone else, providing an early lesson in the transitory nature of romance in the capital; two guests reportedly having sex in the gravel by next door's basement; and me taking a 5 a.m. walk, watching the dustbin men begin their early morning rounds and feeling like Tom Waits yet again.

No one ever washed up in the flat. It was nice, it was central, it couldn't last. As November approached, we attempted to negotiate with Mr Draper about renewing the holiday let. We had at least paid our rent on time. Oh no, he said, he had new tenants to come in and that was it, no argument. We had been astonishingly naive. At least Sean and I planned to confront him about the deposit. Julia looked on doubtfully.

Mr Draper produced a clipboard and smiled thinly. 'These curtains will need cleaning,' he announced, 'and this bed linen, and the carpets will need to be industrially hoovered.' About 15 minutes later, he stopped speaking, having outlined a scenario that could not have been more devastating had the house been sprayed with Agent Orange. Sean and I lapsed into a beaten silence as Mr Draper announced we would receive tuppence of our deposit back.

'There, that really told him,' smirked Julia.

It was an early lesson in the rules of renting: a deposit is yours in theory, but is in reality a gift to your landlord. They take it, they bank it, they earn the interest on it and then they say you haven't washed the curtains and they pocket it.

I made some effort to apply for flat-share adverts in the *Standard*, but incredibly most residents seemed reluctant to mix with a man who had a growing collection of Maupassant novels but no job.

Sean and Julia both moved on to university courses, but ultimately found love through the benevolence of Mr Draper providing us a holiday let. They would eventually produce two children called Withheld and Deposit, or something like that. Diane and Jane went on to find somewhere in Ravenscourt Park with a very high ceiling to accommodate their hairstyles.

The November deadline arrived and I was still accommodation-less and feeling desperate. I'd lost that loafing feeling. My life and career plans had just gone from fast forward to rewind and then the tape had somehow got mangled.

Mercifully, Paul and Katie invited me to come and stay at their rented basement until I found a new flat. I was homeless, unemployed and kipping in a kitchen. Apart from that, everything else was fine.

THE YOUNG ONES

MORTGAGE PROSPECTS: The applicant has no discernible hope of receiving a mortgage offer while unemployed and of no fixed abode. Despite a university degree, he appears to have no career plan in an era of mass unemployment and his malodorous socks are stinking out the kitchen in which he is dossing. He needs to get on his bike and pick up a photocopy of the Capital Flat-share list from the reception at Capital Radio.

AVERAGE HOUSE PRICE IN GREATER LONDON: £36,594

3. Down and Out in W6

Tabor Road, Hammersmith, London W6
December 1982 to May 1983

Hammersmith was my *Notes from Underground* period. While reading Dostoevsky (in the black-spined Penguin Classic edition, of course) in my new basement flat, it felt like I was his nameless anti-hero.

I was a sick man, I was an angry man, I was an unattractive man, I was a literary pseud and I thought there might be something wrong with my liver. At times, it was more *Crime and Punishment* as, like Raskolnikov, I pondered murdering the people who kept interviewing me for teacher training courses and turning me down.

After being evicted from Comeragh Road, I'd spent five weeks sleeping in Paul and Katie's kitchen. There was a reasonably comfy sofa in there, so my nights were fairly untroubled. At weekends, I'd go home to my parents' to try and give Paul and Katie some privacy. Not that they saw too much of me: most nights my DM shoes were marching along wind-strewn autumnal streets looking at potential flat-shares. Dr. Martens' soles might have been oil, fat, acid, petrol and alkali resistant, but would they be flat-hunting resistant too? I doubted it. There were no shoes in existence that could keep pace with a man intent on going through every flat-share ad in the *Standard*.

Just as it seemed that a man with no job, no girlfriend and no home stood as much chance of finding a flat-share as Michael Foot did of being elected, I answered an ad in the Capital Flat-share list for a place in a basement in Hammersmith.

Bizarrely, the very fact that I was signing on got me the flat. After walking down into the basement, I was interviewed by Phil, a Brummie graduate with no fixed career plans, which for me was always a good sign. The people who'd left university with no idea of what they wanted to do were invariably much nicer than the arrogant twits who had everything mapped out and would end up being millionaires, Cabinet ministers or spin doctors.

Phil had just found the flat and needed someone to move into the back room to share the rent. He was signing on as well and, once we discovered that we both liked football (he was a West Brom fan) and music (New Order's 'Blue Monday' was never off his turntable), the room was mine.

Living in a basement was no problem. I had spent time in Paul and Katie's basement, so by the time I reached Tabor Road I was starting to get used to a semi-troglodyte existence. There was no lounge, but Phil had a telly and insisted we use his room for evenings of watching *The Young Ones*, the anarchic new comedy about student house-sharing. There was also a reasonably sized kitchen at the back of the flat, and a garden full of builder's rubble and a small expanse of tundra.

Life on the dole was certainly improving my literary knowledge. Inspired by my time with Sean in Comeragh Road, I was devouring classics: Dostoevsky, Turgenev, Flaubert, Hesse, anything that was foreign and sounded intellectual. If you combined this with the fact that I had purchased a £2.99 tweed overcoat from a charity shop and was playing 'Atmosphere' by Joy Division on my JVC turntable, everything about my persona must have screamed sad, posy post-student git. Clearly this way of life could not be sustainable unless you were Morrissey (who would later make a two-decade career out of it).

Much of my reading was done in a comfy armchair in the above-freezing temperatures of Hammersmith library. The need for warmth was partly because Phil and I were both signing on. Also because the slat windows in my bedroom let in huge waves of arctic air. These louvres were particularly maddening as even when they were closed they left a half-inch gap at the top of the window. The only effective method of insulation was to stuff a couple of old copies of *The Guardian* into the gap. Whoever invented louvres should be tied up and forced to listen to Dire Straits albums for weeks on end. They were probably perfect for Seville, but in Hammersmith they were insane.

The panes of glass were easy for burglars to slide out, too, particularly in a basement flat such as ours – although any thief encountering my piles of used socks and knackered old Elvis Costello tapes would surely have detected the malodorous whiff of post-student poverty and scarpered.

Our landlord Sanjay was perpetually promising to do some work on the flat but, like most landlords, he presided over an empire of property that was always waiting for some form of refurbishment. As landlords go, though, Sanjay was a top man. For a start, he didn't bother to count the rent. He was happy to receive our dues in cash every few weeks, so Phil and I would simply give him three weeks' rent instead of four and he'd appear eminently happy with a wad of notes.

He must have known, of course, but Sanjay seemed to regard us as surrogate sons. He would breeze into the house with infectious cheer, greet his 'boys' and offer to send his cousin round to fix the malfunctioning loo. The fact that we were signing on didn't worry him. In addition to not collecting all the rent, he started to offer Phil odd jobs on house refurbishments in south London. Compared to the likes of Alexei Sayle's Mr Balowski in *The Young Ones*, Sanjay was the greatest landlord ever.

Hammersmith roundabout might have been perpetually busy with traffic heading in and out of London on the A4, and only negotiable by subways, but a few blocks away Tabor Road had a sedate feel to it. Bordered by the busy roads of Hammersmith and Shepherds Bush, the houses in what the estate agents were already trying to market as 'Brackenbury Village' had a distinctly cottagey vibe. A disused church that had been turned into a private home and the Godolphin & Latymer School for posh girls added to the rustic ambience. The houses in Tabor Road were two-storey and had the pleasing yellowy-green sheen of London brickwork. Only taste was not landlord Sanjay's greatest asset: our house had been daubed in cream paint, giving it a cheap pebbledash effect. His renovations were also slow to make any progress. In the course of writing this book, I returned to Tabor Road to discover the door open, a radio blaring inside and the sound of a drill. All the flats were empty and it was almost exactly as it was back in 1982. I have no idea if Sanjay is still the landlord, but it would be no surprise to see him promising immediate renovations and neglecting to collect the rent in full.

A couple of weeks after moving in, I found employment – as a Christmas postman in Kensington High Street. At last, here was an effective use for my Dexys Midnight Runners-style donkey jacket and DM shoes – only the job involved a horribly early start at five o'clock. Kensington High Street would be full of clubbers returning home as the world's unlikeliest and most soporific postman shuffled past in his *Mean Streets* gear on his way to work. This wasn't the sort of thing they'd suggested at all those university careers seminars, but it was fun. Once you mastered the letter boxes that could snap your fingers off, it was easy and rewarding work – and there were marvellous fried breakfasts with toast and sausages saturated in cooked tomatoes to follow in the Post Office canteen. Then, for the rest of the day, I was free to read Penguin Classics.

The arrival of 1983 brought with it the familiar sensation of being a man out of time, at least in the waged world, as unemployment hit me again. At the University of London careers office, I was asked to write a short employment history; the problem was that I had no 'career' history. So far, I'd been a barman, shop assistant, form shuffler, postman and failed Flaubert reader. There was an interview for a place at a teacher training course in Nottingham, which I failed. With unemployment figures continuing to lurk around the three million mark, it seemed that every graduate in the country wanted to be an English teacher and the demand for places was huge. Perhaps the interviewers sensed that I longed to be Elvis Costello far more than I did John Alderton in *Please, Sir!*

DOWN AND OUT IN W6

It wasn't as if I even wanted their jobs; writing was my goal, but I just didn't know how to get there. Every Monday, there was the familiar scan through the creative and media job pages of *The Guardian*. I'd read about posts requiring experience, assertiveness and a Ph.D. in pomposity, only to despair and then use them to stuff the gaps in my bedroom window.

So, it was back to a life of being down and out in W6, reading Flaubert, Nietzsche and Hesse in the library, visiting the Record and Tape Exchange on Goldhawk Road and using the money I'd earned being a postie to subsidise my social life. Oh, and nicking bricks from a nearby building site with Phil to help create makeshift bookcases. You could probably get a TV design show on the basis of such ingenuity today.

On Wednesday nights, a group of us would often gather at Paul and Katie's flat in Notting Hill to watch *Boys from the Blackstuff*, a series by Alan Bleasdale exposing the terrible reality of unemployment in Liverpool. This was in pre-video days when television programmes were an event. We watched the 'Yosser's Story' episode in awe and knew then that no one would ever elect a Conservative government again.

Sometimes Phil and I would search for a decent pub in the backstreets of Hammersmith. We'd probably still be searching if we were there now. The pubs by the river, such as the Dove and Blue Anchor, were promising but packed with tourists; everything away from the main arteries seemed dead. Or I'd go and visit Sean's sister Dee in Earls Court, where she and her flatmate Irene had colonised a pub called the Drayton Arms. Nearby was another boozer called the Colherne, where gay men with moustaches wearing leather gear would stand on the pavements drinking. These were not earnest gay activists like Tom Robinson. They all looked like the biker from the Village People. In 1983, it was strange to see men being so openly gay; to me it all seemed part of London's fascinating burlesque. *The Sun* would have hated it, though: at the time, the tabloid was at its most rabidly homophobic.

One night I travelled over the river to meet my old school mate and Labour Party activist, Nick, for a post-Bermondsey by-election drink in the Labour Club. The mood was morose among the activists; Labour was losing safe seats. Candidate Peter Tatchell had been ridiculed in every way by the tabloids and even had his picture touched up to make it look like he was wearing make-up. Simon Hughes had eventually won the seat for the Liberals. Tatchell then outed himself and became a gay activist.

Sanjay had extended his hospitality to Phil's mate Kate and her boyfriend Andrei, who were now renting the upstairs flat. Kate was a wonderful character who could make a Brummie accent seem sexy. Phil used to go out with her; indeed, it was mystifying to me why they had ever split up. Kate had a proper job in publishing and knew people like agents. Whenever she discussed serious literary concepts, her voice deepened in tone. When gazed at through the eyes of an unemployed writer with a penchant for Sartre's *Nausea*, she was the most glamorous person in Hammersmith.

Why were there not more women like Kate available? And if they were out there, why were they ignoring an unemployed man with questionable personal hygiene, a collection of quality literature and a long overcoat? It's still as mystifying today as it was then.

Kate and Andrei had a friend in a long Mac called Austin who spent every evening recording bootlegs of gigs with a handheld cassette player. Kate and Andrei spent a lot of time enthusing about his Test Department bootlegs. (Test Department were a lot of men banging bits of metal together, but it seemed fashionable back then.)

Hammersmith Odeon was close too and Phil, Kate, Andrei and I once saw Soft Cell play there. Martin Fry, Siouxsie Sioux, Steve Severin, Budgie, Blancmange, Clare Grogan and Kim Wilde were all there. And so too, in trendy new black denim jeans, was Pete May, just like Rik in *The Young Ones*, the People's Poet of Hammersmith, waiting to be discovered and taken away from his tainted love of basement flats.

Our home was needing a bit more than a Soft Cell, though. Back at the flat it was like a scene from a Graham Greene story, 'The Turd Man'. Our sewage system was sending turds back to the top of the lavatory bowl with effortless economy. Sanjay sent some men who dug up most of the garden while Phil and I tipped buckets of poo onto the wasteland that used to be a garden, creating a fragrant aroma that wafted back through my draught-ridden slat window. Eventually, the fault was cleared, but only after we had moved half of Hammersmith's excrement from out of our khazi.

The Wednesday morning signing-on ritual was the biggest event in my life at that time. It meant an early start as I had to be at the DHSS office by 10 a.m. In March, however, two events occurred that were to change my life.

First, Paul and I and another friend called Paul decided to start a fanzine entitled *Notes from Underground*. We were Dostoevsky readers and all of W6 was going to know it. Copyright played no part in our thinking; other people's work was there for us to use. If we wanted a picture, we simply cut it out of the *NME*. We typed our copy on ancient typewriters and then simply glued it to a piece of A4 paper and made the headlines with Letraset. We then photocopied the pages at work, stapled them together and had a fanzine produced at virtually no cost.

There were exciting new things called cabaret clubs opening up, which had pleasing associations of Sally Bowles-meets-*City Limits* readers. There were new alternative 'ranting poets' too, like 'Seething Wells' (later to be Steven Wells of the *NME*) and Attila the Stockbroker. Visiting the Sol Y Sombra club in the West End, we met a poet called Joolz who said we could use her work.

Our first issues contained my features on Dexys and John Cooper Clarke, my own and Attila's poems, a piece on 'Bermondsey's Bingo By-election' and a 'Curry House of the Month' section by Paul, a piece on CND by the other Paul, a letter from Guatemala dispatched by our school pal Crispin, who was travelling around South America on a bike, a professional gambler's manifesto by Kevin from our Rose Valley days in Brentwood and live reviews of Simple Minds and Nick Cave by Kate, New Order by Phil and the Stranglers by Sean.

It might have only been a photocopied fanzine, but at last I was doing what I wanted – writing. For us it was the late twentieth-century equivalent of Thomas Paine's political pamphlets merged with the literary importance of Proust.

We placed ten copies each in a number of London's alternative bookshops such as Compendium in Camden Town and the place at Wood Green that Alan and Bronwyn frequented, and it was also available through mail order. Whenever we went to a cabaret evening, we'd sell copies on the street too. We were soon part of a circuit. Another fanzine writer flogging his mag from a plastic bag was a northerner called James Brown who was later to end up editing lads' mag *Loaded*.

Buoyed by the success of the fanzine, other aspects of my life changed too. After nearly three years of lying low, in March 2003 the big one finally arrived. Only it came in the form of a job at the National Dairy Council (NDC). Paul was leaving his job there to work at the Milk Marketing Board and had mentioned to his boss that he had a mate who needed a job. One interview later, I was in, with no other candidates involved in the selection process. After all those years of applying for jobs from the poncy *Guardian* creative and media section, one arrived from something as simple as a bit of cronyism.

I'm not sure that Kevin Rowland would have accepted a job publicising milk, cheese and yogurt (that is, incidentally, the favoured industry version of the spelling of yogurt, rather than the commonly used 'yoghurt'), but my post as an editorial assistant in the press office was easy work. It involved scanning the morning papers for references to milk, cream and cheese (you'll never know how often *The Sun* used the word 'pinta' in 1983, but I do). There were some cuttings to file, a little general helping of other members of staff in the press office and the odd film to show to visitors to the NDC, and that was about it.

The whole place had the feel of Sunshine Desserts about it, but someone had to promote dairy products and it was paying me £6,500 p.a. My mum and dad were delighted; at last I had a 'permanent, pensionable job'.

My new position as a man with a permanent, pensionable job also meant that I could re-evaluate my accommodation options. In the transitory world of London lettings, you're always searching for that something extra.

DOWN AND OUT IN W6

By this time, Phil was doing numerous painting jobs for Sanjay and often at home watching TV in the evenings, enthusing about a new soap opera called *Brookside*. He was a sociable man and a decent bloke, but sometimes I missed my privacy, just wanting to be alone to write or read rather than feeling obliged to join Phil in his room next door. I decided that a house with a lounge would be a better option. And maybe somewhere that wasn't a basement, and had a working window and sewage disposal system would be nice.

This took much longer than expected. Sanjay was, of course, infinitely sad to learn that I might be leaving and insisted on driving me to another of his properties in Goldhawk Road, but since it was basically a bedsit, I declined. So, using a combination of the *Standard*, the Capital Flat-share list and a variety of newsagents' windows, the search began. A place advertised in the *Standard* at West Kensington had already gone; at Shepherds Bush, one flat had a live-in landlady and the other had already been given to someone else; East Finchley was just too far out and suburban, and had Margaret Thatcher as an MP; North End Road, W6, I didn't get; West Kensington, again, was crap and I got soaked getting there; at Earls Court, two places had gone and the people were awful at the third; at Fulham Palace Road, the room was minute; Ladbroke Grove rejected me.

Flat-hunting in London was like something from a Thomas Hardy novel; you always arrived too late to prevent tragedy. You'd walk halfway across the capital in the rain to find the room you were after had gone five minutes earlier. How old Thomas would have loved the Capital Flat-share list as a metaphor for the unfeeling cosmos and the lack of a benevolent deity.

Finally, my search took me to a place above a building society in Parsons Green and, incredibly, the two other tenants invited me to join them. I wasn't too sure about them, but it was a spacious flat set on two storeys with a huge lounge and it was such a relief to at last feel wanted in flatland that I accepted. Which was to prove a massive mistake.

RENT BOY

MORTGAGE PROSPECTS: At last, the applicant has a permanent, pensionable job. He is showing signs of growing up and calming down and ending his ridiculous fixation with itinerant flat-sharing and hopeless dreams of literary conquest that certainly won't pay the mortgage, ever. Providing he commits himself to promoting milk, cream and cheese for the rest of his life and, of course, passes his three-month probationary period at the NDC, he may eventually save enough money for a one-bedroom flat in deepest south London.

AVERAGE HOUSE PRICE IN GREATER LONDON: £42,486

4. No Sloane Unturned

Fulham Road, Parsons Green, London SW6
May 1983 to May 1984

My house had been sacked by Goths. Someone had been sick both in the front room and on the doorstep. The Sunday joint had been stolen from the fridge. There was bubble bath down the loo. The speakers had blown. There were cigarette burns on the carpet. Half-full cans, paper cups of stale spirits, beer and dog-ends littered the house like the debris from some apocalyptic battle of SW6. As a way of endearing myself to my Sloane Ranger flatmates, it was not ideal.

It was a decent house: three storeys set above a building society on the Fulham Road. The living room was spacious and my bedroom was at the rear, so the noise of traffic and raucous restaurant customers returning along the Fulham Road would not be too disruptive. The landlord and landlady were a married couple from Putney, an ex-policeman called Lance and his wife Jane. They were still technically the tenants of the property, so we had to pay them the rent cash-in-hand and never mention to the real landlords that they had moved out.

When interviewed for the vacant room, I had some qualms about the two other tenants. Richard was an ex-public schoolboy now working for a bank who seemed inoffensive, if somewhat straight. (Any 24 year old who listed his main hobby as DIY was surely heading for premature Richard Briersdom, even if he did have a

45

nice-seeming girlfriend who was a nurse.) Selena, who worked for an embassy, gave the impression of being somewhat lace-curtain in her outlook, but was friendly enough at that first meeting.

They wanted me and, crucially, there was another room in the house up for rent in a month's time. Get a decent flatmate in there and the house would be fine, I reasoned. The fact that it was spacious and it had a lounge, and the sheer shock of being accepted for a flat-share, had all conspired to make me take the room. It was only later that I realised they had probably accepted me because they were impressed by a man who worked for the National Dairy Council and had devoted his life to promoting milk, cream, cheese and yogurt. They'd missed the decadent party-goer, the Elvis Costello lover, the CND-badge-wearer bit entirely.

There were a few pockets of council housing in Fulham, but it was now invariably populated by the posh. As an indicator, a short walk from our flat at Parsons Green was the White Horse, a pub which specialised in roast beef Sunday lunches for men in rugby shirts and horsey women.

On 10 June 1983, the morning of Margaret Thatcher's election victory, I scanned the gleeful faces on the Tube in disbelief. These people were happy to live in Fulham, but had no comprehension that just over Battersea Bridge there was real poverty. They didn't want to hear about unemployment in Liverpool or Newcastle. I was still picturing comedian Kenny Everett at a Tory election rally with his tired bad-taste jokes like 'Kick Michael Foot's stick away!' as I gazed at the striped shirts and upturned collars. Here were people glorying in an old man's defeat. Greed had won again.

Parsons Green had its good points: it was close to Thameside walks at Putney Bridge and Bishops Park on Fulham Palace Road, and there were plenty of restaurants on the Fulham Road; but back then, England seemed like it was at war. You were either for Margaret Thatcher or against her, and these were not my people.

My problems at home began when the final bedroom was let. *The Sloane Ranger's Handbook* by Peter York and Ann Barr had just been published and Parsons Green seemed to be their habitat familiar. While commuting to the Dairy Council, I'd stand waiting for the

District Line train feeling like the only man ever to pass through Parsons Green station without a Barbour or a copy of *The Times*. And I was undoubtedly the only man there who would have instantly associated the word Marlborough with cigarettes and not a school.

A legal secretary called Kirsty arrived to be interviewed for the vacant room. She was wearing the authentic Sloane uniform of puffa jacket, striped shirt with upturned collar and pearls. Of course, nobody who was really upper class would follow the Sloane stereotype so exactly; Kirsty was classic lower-middle class *Daily Mail*-reading material. Somehow, I sensed we wouldn't get on. The other two loved her and immediately invited her to move in.

Our relationship got off to a dodgy start when I arrived home at 11.30 on a Sunday morning, severely hungover after a dissolute party and some rare love action, to find Kirsty moving her things in. She knew then that I was a left-wing reprobate who didn't read the *Daily Mail*.

Nor was she impressed when I told her in the kitchen that I was going on a CND rally to Hyde Park. 'Do they really know what they're marching for?' she asked. What did she know about the absurdities of nuclear stockpiling and the Cold War? Like Tom Robinson, we were talking 'bout the Third World War, baby. The arms race between America and Russia had resulted in enough nuclear weapons being created to destroy the planet 300 times over. In five years, Neil Kinnock would be in power, a man who would never go back on his commitment to taking us out of the global arms race that would end in mutually assured destruction.

Enid Blyton's *The Famous Five* had just been parodied on Channel 4 by *The Comic Strip Presents* but to my no doubt extremely intolerant eyes, it seemed that Kirsty wanted to model herself on the originals. She didn't really know many people in London and wanted picnics and dinner parties and evenings cooking beef bourguignon. She heartily disapproved of my habit of going to my room and playing Elvis Costello's *Punch the Clock* or working on the pages of my fanzine. Kirsty wanted full-scale house involvement.

As the hottest summer for 300 years hit London (so the tabloids claimed), I was sweltering at house gatherings. Kirsty would arbitrarily announce a meeting to discuss the state of the stairs or any other of her 27 complaints. Selena was by then teaming up with her. The tyranny of the house rota was introduced. It was a hugely complicated wall chart which covered stair duties, mopping, bathroom cleaning, hoovering and no doubt polishing your boots with a toothbrush.

Along with the rota came the house kitty for the instant coffee and dodgy white bread in the kitchen. These were good ideas in principle, but they were pursued with all the zealotry of Year Zero Pol Pot enthusiasts. Invariably, when something was wrong, Kirsty and Selena would blame me. I was once rebuked for agreeing to vacuum the stairs, but without enough enthusiasm in my voice. 'It's not a favour, it's an obligation!' ranted Selena.

When Kirsty started labelling her food in the fridge and marking the level of her shampoo in the bathroom, I knew just how petty things had become with the Khmer Rouge of SW6. Or I'd find my towel flung on the landing on the grounds that it was a health and safety hazard, or be harangued over a post-shaving bristle-in-the-sink incident.

Yes, yes, yes, I was a bloke and no doubt crap at most chores. But in mitigation, I did always try to wash up after I'd cooked, attempted to do my share of the hoovering and put my money in the house kitty. Part of the problem was that I was rarely in. Thanks to three successive house-shares and a job, my social circle had expanded. Paul and Katie were still around, doing a circuit of bars and clubs in Notting Hill, and so were Phil, Kate and Andrei, Sean, Julia, Diane and Jane from Comeragh Road and Sean's sister Dee.

Diane and Jane were still hanging out in the Moscow Arms at Notting Hill, with Psychedelic Furs fans with huge spiky multi-coloured hair. They're probably all members of Rotary Clubs now, but in the early '80s, Paul, Katie and I would go there just for the spectacle and the best jukebox in London. Despite being a housing misfit and dairy magnate, there were plenty of friends around and most nights I'd go out after work seeking pubs, bars, gigs and parties. It now seemed a huge mistake ever to have left the basement in Hammersmith.

Everything might have been easier with a girlfriend, of course. But that involved romancing the phone. The phone numbers of available women were mystic digits to me. It would take several coffees and many minutes of procrastination before picking up the receiver and dialling that number.

Rejection was embarrassing and excruciating and could come in many forms: 'Who are you?' meant she must have been very drunk indeed when she gave you her phone number; 'I've got someone here. I'll ring you back' meant she never would. Sometimes you'd hear a voice shouting to a beleaguered flatmate, 'I'm not in!' Or one of my intended amour's flatmates would announce 'She's in the bath!' There must have been a lot of very clean young women in London, as they were nearly always in the bath. My disastrous dating attempts kept British Telecom in profits throughout the early '80s.

Work at the Dairy Council was almost a welcome release from the problems at home. It was an organisation full of Dickensian misfits and marvellous characters. A journalist called Rick had been charged with producing *Dairy Mirror*, the NDC's pulsating monthly paper for the industry. (One legendary issue had managed to describe 'brick-shaped cheeses' as 'prick-shaped cheeses' after a typographical gremlin had crept in. No one had noticed until we were instructed to send a grovelling letter of apology to numerous dairy industry stalwarts and several MPs.) In his mid-30s, Rick lived at home with his mother in Brighton and was often on the phone whispering to her. 'PWW!' he'd utter at me in a furtive tone, 'that's what my mother thinks I am, a playboy of the western world.'

Rick had two great hobbies. The first was what he referred to as 'the quadrupeds'. After emerging sweaty-browed from the bookies at lunchtime, he'd complain that he 'just hadn't got enough ammo' for the type of gambling operation he required. His other pastime was his 'stony friends'. He'd pull open a desk drawer to show me a newly acquired ammonite or a map of a proposed new pipeline in Sussex. At other times, he'd tell me of the woman he'd met at the fossil shop – 'anthropologist, 38, no attachments' – in his peculiar, conspiratorial style.

National Dairy Council photographer Peter Stepto was a 60-year-old former Fleet Street legend who had once worked for the *Daily Mirror*, always available with his tale about dying for a pee while stuck up a gantry at the Queen's coronation in 1953. Why the NDC needed an in-house photographer was never clear. This was in the days before the world had gone freelance, mind you.

Each morning, Peter would arrive from Brighton at 10.30 or 11 a.m. with the clatter of bags and camera cases falling to the floor, saying something like, 'I've been travelling on that bloody line for 30 years and I've never known a single week pass without a train being late. The guard comes down the train and tells us "I'm sorry. There will be a delay because the train has lost a shoe," and I say "So did Cinderella, but at least she got to the ball on time!"' He was a star and a master of bad puns who taught me everything I know about writing groan-inducing headlines. Peter maintained that 'the pun was mightier than the sword'. He seconded my application to join the National Union of Journalists and allowed me to be his touchline assistant while taking pictures at Milk Cup games.

A refined and friendly man called Charles was in charge of sponsorships and spent his whole life in flustered pursuit of walkabout cheeses. A rotund, middle-aged woman whom Terry, our grimy-looking maintenance man, had named Garden Gnome was responsible for placing dairy recipes in women's magazines.

The press office was overseen by Mr Hill (your boss didn't have a first name, even in 1983) or, as Rick referred to him, 'the old boy'. He was a decent enough man, who, at one point, had been the editor of a top magazine, but was now heading towards retirement at 65. His friendly and efficient secretary, Margaret, had been there since the dawn of the dairy industry and kept the whole office going.

It was a bizarre job, involving a little press work, occasionally tackling a temperamental projector to show some ancient dairy films to visiting parties of pensioners, and much carting of giant milk bottles around in the back of the company motor. I was the dairy industry's version of Arthur Daley's odd-job man, Terence McCann. There were also several NDC sponsorships. That summer saw me pursuing the Milk Race cyclists through Cheddar Gorge with Charles, handing out 'pintas' to a grateful Bryan Robson and Norman Whiteside at the FA Cup final and learning how to drive a milk float that needed to be delivered back to its depot from the Royal Exchange.

Oh, and then there was the famous NDC-sponsored Operation Skyquest. This was a sponsored hot-air balloon with 'I've gotta lotta bottle!' emblazoned on its side. It was bidding to break the world hot-air balloon altitude record. At its launch in Watton, Norfolk, pilot Per Lindstrand was left comically suspended from a guy rope as the rogue balloon broke free from its mooring and collapsed, according to one national paper, 'like a deflated French letter'. Rick at the *Dairy Mirror* wrote of 'impish winds' as he tried to disguise the fiasco. Peter Stepto called it a piece of 'Watton luck'.

It was while I was at the Dairy Council that it first became apparent that everyone had become obsessed with the London housing market. Garden Gnome began telling me that there were some building societies offering 100 per cent mortgages and that I really should try to get on the property ladder. This seemed vaguely ridiculous. Mortgages were for people who were old and knew what they wanted to do. Nor was my salary that large. And besides, my dad said that property prices were ridiculously high. I answered with something about not wanting to be trapped working forever and Margaret replied with 'What else is there to do?' A good question, but I didn't envisage a lifetime devoted to dairy produce, even if the NDC was very useful for furtively photocopying a few extra pages of my fanzine.

Paul and Katie, however, were now buying a flat in Notting Hill, aided by a discounted mortgage through the bank where Katie worked. If I ever found the right career or even someone to share my life and mortgage payments with, then perhaps I should be sensible and consider buying.

By the start of 1984, I was staying out as much as I could rather than tolerate the icy atmosphere in Parsons Green. Elvis Costello gigs at the Hammersmith Odeon and Gary Glitter (who was a cult figure to the post-student generation that grew up with his glam rock singles) at the Palais helped my morale, even if neither of them turned up at my house meetings to support me in person.

At one house meeting, Kirsty suggested that I didn't fit in. Her smugness was appalling. I was paying rent just like the rest of them. I didn't expect her to fit in with my lifestyle so why should she expect me to fit in with hers? Later that night, I overhead the others talking in the living room and caught Kirsty saying 'He'd be more at home with layabouts and squatters!' She was right, of course. In fact, I imagined a spell staying at the house of Dennis Nilsen, who had just been on trial for murdering and dismembering up to 16 down-and-outs at his bedsit in Muswell Hill, would have been preferable to life in Parsons Green.

Still, at one house meeting my idea of holding a party had been somewhat surprisingly accepted. So at least there would be a little mileage out of the house as a party venue before my seemingly inevitable exit from the land of stand-up collars.

The party was scheduled for the first Saturday in February 1984 and all my London and Essex friends and acquaintances were invited. The house could have coped with that. Only I'd also invited Goths Diane and Jane, whose speciality was to pass any party address around the whole of the Moscow Arms.

First, there was a session in the White Horse and then a march back to my front room and on with the party tape. Paul and Katie arrived and were amazed to find a queue outside the house stretching all the way round onto the Fulham Road. About 200 Goths had surged out of the Moscow Arms and invaded Fulham Road. Everyone else I knew in London had turned up too. Phil, Kate and Andrei from Hammersmith were there, and Julia, several of Paul and Katie's friends and some of my old mates from my university days as well.

It all became unstoppable. The front room seemed to be vibrating up and down. One out-of-it reveller sat on the stairs all evening with his head in his hands, oblivious to those walking over him. An array of black-haired female Goths in fingerless gloves helped create an air of Dickensian libation. There were cries of 'Leader! Leader!' when Gary Glitter's song came on my party tape, causing mayhem. The Beatles' 'Twist and Shout', 'Pretty in Pink' by the Furs, 'London Calling', the huge bass lines of The Clash's 'Armagideon Time' . . .

Hell, it was all too successful. My flatmates arrived back from dinner and were stunned by the numbers but powerless to stem the waves of Goths being launched at west London from the Moscow. Maggie Thatcher was right, the Moscow legions were indeed a threat to civilised life in all Western democracies.

At 4 a.m., I gave up and crashed out. I awoke at around 8 a.m. to find five other people in my room and Selena haranguing me about the dossers in the sitting room. Hasty hungover evictions took place as I frantically tried to clean the place up. There was detritus everywhere – dog-ends, half-empty cans, vomit on the doorstep and down the back of the sofa. The hi-fi system was suffering from a blown speaker, but I could handle that. Only it got worse. There were bubbles flooding from the loo – which had become the sort of foaming mass not seen since 'Fury of the Deep' in *Doctor Who* – and lipstick writing on the mirror. Then Richard informed me that the house Sunday joint had been stolen from out of the fridge. What sort of person takes raw meat home with them? A pillaging Visigoth, I suppose. Kirsty announced that her £12 bottle of champagne had gone, too.

Jesus Christ. If they want cleaning up, they're going to get it. I offered Kirsty cash compensation for the champagne as she stood there oozing moral superiority. There was much scrubbing of floors, emptying of cans, clearing up of vomit, discreet placing of the sofa over cigarette burns and opening of windows. Four hours later, it looked almost presentable, even if my head did feel like it had Kirsty shouting at amp mark eleven somewhere inside it. Incredibly, landlords Lance and Jane then turned up at midday for an impromptu visit and complimented us on how neat the house looked.

The next day was Paul's birthday and before a curry we searched the Moscow Arms, but there was no sign of the missing joint. The party had created a huge amount of anecdotes and it was always that post-party dissection of events that I found most enjoyable. Especially since at least 200 people now owed me a riotous bash. Ha! I was on the London party circuit forevermore.

Back at Fulham Road, the others seemed reasonably good humoured about the party. But it was only a pause in our conflict. Perhaps they were just wary of the forces of scarlet-barneted spikiness I could muster from the Moscow Arms.

Slowly the barbs started coming, such as when a friend who stayed the night on my floor had the audacity to use the bathroom in the morning at Kirsty's usual time. *The Prisoner* was being repeated on Channel 4 and I was starting to feel more and more like Patrick McGoohan, only with Rover replaced by bouncing Sloanes in puffa jackets.

Two weeks later, I arrived home just before midnight to the sound of the others holding some sort of soirée in the living room. After trudging up the stairs to my room, I discovered that the house kitty jar was on my bed along with an empty jar of instant coffee. It wasn't an early attempt at seduction in the style of the Gold Blend adverts – there was a hastily scrawled note beside it reading: 'I want you out of here and so do all of us. You contribute nothing to this house! I am not your nursemaid or your fucking mother! Just fucking well leave! Kirsty.' Apart from that she seemed to quite like me.

It's not often that I lose my temper – about once every 15 years, in fact – but this, as Dennis Waterman might have put it in *Minder*, was way out of order. For ten or fifteen minutes, I sat on my bed trying to breathe calmly.

Then I ran downstairs, kicked open the sitting room door, waved the note in the air like a belligerent version of Neville Chamberlain and shouted out that Kirsty was a spoilt child and a pseudo Sloane Ranger and that I always washed up after every meal I ate in the kitchen and that if I chose to go out and leave them to get on with their lives then I wasn't hurting anyone and she was sick and intolerant and who was she to send fucking notes full of fucking swearwords anyway? Personally, I thought it was quite a measured response.

It was something that every tenant has experienced at some

stage: complete and irretrievable breakdown with their housemates. Joy Division were wrong: it was not love that would tear us apart but house-sharing. At least Kirsty looked slightly embarrassed by this tirade in front of her friends.

That night, I could hardly sleep for rage and hurt. Of course, running away wouldn't solve anything, but I did it anyway. For the next 15 nights, I kipped on friends' floors and sofas using a combination of Paul and Katie, Julia, my parents in Essex and an all-night party where I became exactly the kind of human debris that I'd had to throw out of my own house so recently.

While leading this peripatetic lifestyle, I started looking at houses and flats, reflecting that at last I had become the sort of impoverished, rootless Dostoevsky-like character I'd fantasised about being while living in Hammersmith. The Pope might have just said that he forgave the man who shot him, but that was more than I could do with Kirsty.

At lunchtimes, I'd buy the *Standard* or pick up the Capital Flat-share list. Wearily walking winter streets after work, SW6's itinerant Sloane refugee surveyed places in Fulham (twice), Hammersmith, Putney (twice), Ravenscourt Park, Shepherds Bush, Notting Hill (twice), Clapham (four times) and Islington – fourteen in total. A flat of my own was what I really needed, of course, but on my salary it was unaffordable.

Why were flats so difficult to find in London? It was a combination of factors: people moving from the depressed North to the affluent South in search of jobs; the virtual abandonment of council-house building and the fact that councils were not allowed to use the capital receipts from council-house sales to build more housing; fewer people wanting to be landlords when they could sit on a property and watch it increase in value by the month; and a government that just didn't seem to care if you couldn't afford to buy a home.

By now, I had surely acquired the Knowledge necessary to become a cabbie, but still had no flat. My bedtime reading was the London A–Z. It might have been a bit short on plot, but it was a book that could transport you into new and dangerous regions of the psyche.

At night, it was usual to arrive in a distant part of London to find myself one of twenty-four applicants with five minutes to sell myself to four prospective flatmates I was pretty certain I didn't like. Or find the place had already gone, or it was a horribly small room, or had a live-in landlord. A depressed and exhausted rough sleeper working in the milk industry did not seem to be anyone's idea of the perfect flatmate.

After 15 days of exile, I received a phone call at work from Selena. She was strangely conciliatory and explained that none of the others had known about the note Kirsty had sent me and that they had all told her she had gone way too far. She asked me to come back to my room. It felt like a victory of sorts as I returned for a house meeting where Kirsty apologised and I explained that although I wasn't always in, I would try to contribute to the house as much as possible. Richard, his girlfriend Sandie and Selena seemed quite friendly towards me, while they were cold towards a subdued Kirsty.

A few days after my return, Arthur Scargill decided to attempt similarly militant tactics with Margaret Thatcher and the national miners' strike began. I was possibly the only man ever to be sighted at Parsons Green station wearing a yellow 'Coal Not Dole' sticker. Kirsty hated this, but was for a few weeks forced to remain silent.

The sense of home had been destroyed for me, however, and there was always the likelihood of further trouble once Kirsty regained her confidence. After a short holiday with Julia and two of her friends in Paris – which in the spring sunshine seemed an immensely calm city compared to London – I resolved to start looking for flats again.

Meanwhile, there was a new career to consider – I had been transformed into a giant milk bottle. At the 1984 Milk Cup final between Liverpool and Everton, I successfully donned a giant fibreglass walkabout milk bottle costume with 'I've gotta lotta bottle!' emblazoned on it. The walkabout bottles and cheeses and milk floats performed as part of the Dairy Parade at Wembley, before being pelted with coins and witticisms from thousands of whistling Scousers.

NO SLOANE UNTURNED

Through April and May, there were yet more nocturnal visits to mysterious addresses somewhere on the A–Z. I felt a bit like those men who spend their evenings furtively ringing bells in red-light districts; only at least they gained some passing satisfaction out of their forays. It was back to two-minute interviews to sell myself before the next person in the twenty-strong queue came in. One house-tenant quiz still rankles 20 years on, during which an obnoxious Thatcherite City-type asked me: 'Where do you see yourself in five years' time?' Not living with you, you prat!

There were trips to West Hampstead, Hammersmith, Paddington, Stockwell, Clapham, Queens Park, Westbourne Park, Parsons Green, Wandsworth, Clapham, Hammersmith, North Clapham, Fulham, Clapham (again), West Kensington and West Hampstead (again). It was a blur of small rooms with paper walls, landladies with more regulations than the DHSS, communal cooking rotas, cacophonous rooms on main roads and small rooms lodging with Norman Tebbit fans – not that anyone offered me a room anyway.

Application number 23 was particularly cruel. It was a flat in Wandsworth with people I liked. The house leader phoned to offer me the room and I immediately accepted. At last, I could enjoy the sleep of the just housed. Only the next day she phoned to apologise, saying that she was very sorry but the woman who had originally been offered it had changed her mind. Great.

That May, a passionate young singer called Billy Bragg played at the London School of Economics and I was mesmerised by his set. He looked like he'd emerged straight from his front room and seemed to encapsulate my years on the dole in songs like 'To Have and Have Not'. 'New England' was also strangely relevant in that, like Billy, I didn't want to change the world, I was just looking for another flat.

But I was not going to be defeated. In true Norman Tebbit-style, I'd got on my bike and looked for a flat. In fact, I'd looked at 38 of them. If adverts were no use, then it was time to try word of mouth. Some old friends, Pat and Keith, were moving out of their rented flat in Fulham Broadway to buy in Streatham and suggested that I have a word with the estate agent who was letting the property.

RENT BOY

I visited the estate agent near the Broadway, paid the deposit, gave references and signed the contract. It all seemed too easy and I was mentally too exhausted to even celebrate. I'd seen fires and I'd seen pain, but I never thought I'd see a tenancy agreement again. Like Robert Wyatt, at last I was free. Nothing, absolutely nothing, could ever be as bad as living with Kirsty in Parsons Green. Could it?

MORTGAGE PROSPECTS: The applicant has failed to note the significance of the fact that most of his friends who are couples are now buying properties. Because his salary is relatively low, he appears reluctant to apply for a 100 per cent mortgage in Croydon and still holds bizarre notions of finding satisfying, creative work instead of promoting dairy products. He is expending far too much energy on fanzine-writing, fighting with his flatmates and searching for rented rooms when he should be concentrating on scaling the property ladder. It is our opinion that he is uneconomic and should be closed down.

AVERAGE HOUSE PRICE IN GREATER LONDON: £48,379

5. The Siege of Fulham Broadway

Fulham Broadway, Fulham, London SW6
May 1984 to July 1984

This had to be a record – even by my standards of housing failure. Having moved into the flat on Fulham Broadway on the Saturday, I was queuing up at the Fulham Legal Advice Centre by Monday night.

Two weeks earlier, I'd handed over the deposit and an 'agency fee' to an oleaginous estate agent whom Peter Stepto was later to nickname Mr Rachman, after the notorious slum landlord of the 1960s. Having enjoyed the solitude of a life free from Sloanes in my own flat for a full 48 hours, Rachman phoned me at work to say that there was a problem with the landlord's solicitors clearing my references and would I mind awfully moving out for two weeks. This tale had a distinct nautical whiff to it and I told him that I would not be going anywhere. Where did he expect me to go? Kirsty's room? A riverside bench with all facilities suitable for a non-smoker in Bishops Park? The Legal Advice Centre reassured me that the landlord had little or no case.

Having fought my way through 38 flat viewings to find this one, I was not going to be moved. Ever. The flat was situated above the Asian newsagents on the busy Broadway where the owner worked. Access was gained through a back alley and a set of iron stairs that resembled something from *On the Waterfront*. A large sitting room at the front of the house looked over the Broadway.

At the rear of the flat were a smaller bedroom and a kitchen covered with '60s lino and grease-stained orange wallpaper. It resembled a transport café and was pleasingly kitsch. The wires hanging from a number of electrical fittings resembled something from the interior of *Doctor Who*'s Tardis console and the fridge looked like it could explode at any moment, but everything else appeared to just about work. Upstairs, there was a mysterious half-empty flat in which two nocturnal asylum seekers slept when not working in a nearby kebab shop.

The flat was £50 a week, which I couldn't really afford on my salary. However, I reasoned that if I advertised for a flatmate, the costs could be halved. With me controlling who moved in, there would be no more domestic debacles. So I placed an advert in the Capital Flat-share list, enjoying the sudden role reversal.

Instead of asking the applicants where they saw themselves in five years' time, I stuck to more pertinent questions such as 'What are your views on house rotas?' and 'Are you an anally retentive git?' On revealing that he had once lived in a Land-Rover in Highbury while homeless and that he hated house rotas, a social worker called Ronald was deemed exceptional and recruited immediately. He'd had a similar experience to mine in Parsons Green, only Ronald had shared with militant Socialist Workers Party (SWP) members in Finsbury Park who saw politics as religion and hated him for not embracing the class struggle with as much fervour as them. I explained the problems with the estate agent but he was happy to take a chance and become my flatmate.

Away from the flat, there was plenty happening that summer. One of the bizarre aspects of London at the time was that you could be at a Psychedelic Furs gig at the Hammersmith Odeon one night (where the entire Sunday-joint pilfering clientele of the Moscow Arms had decamped for the evening in a vast swathe of spiked maroon barnets and white faces), then on a demo against South Africa's President Botha visiting the UK a couple of days later.

That June saw a CND rally at Trafalgar Square with the usual 27 speakers who all went on a bit too long, and the Greater London Council (GLC) Jobs for a Change Festival at County Hall. Since

THE SIEGE OF FULHAM BROADWAY

Margaret Thatcher had decided to abolish the GLC, Ken Livingstone had become something of a folk hero to most young Londoners, particularly as he kept putting on free gigs.

Only these were polarised times. During the Redskins' set, the stage was invaded by British National Party (BNP) skinheads who stopped the band from playing. It was a frightening moment. Headliners The Smiths emerged unscathed and the day was redeemed by Billy Bragg, who played a superb set at some personal risk. He ended his set with a breathless speech (and I should know, I still have the bootleg tape) imploring us that: 'There are lots of things to be done this summer, anything to do with the GLC or CND or backing the miners, it's all part of the same struggle against the oncoming tide of totalitarianism from across that river!

'The only way anyone is going to turn back the tide is by getting involved, no matter how small – coming to gigs, going on marches – because as we've already seen this afternoon, the enemy is everywhere! It's not gone anyway. They're not all sitting in their houses, they're all still about just waiting for the opportunity and the start of it all is things like taking away votes at County Hall, crushing the miners, ending trade union power and stopping the Redskins playing! It's all part of the same problem!

'They'll chip away at the miners, they'll chip away at County Hall and eventually when they come for you normal people, there won't be nobody left to defend you any more. So just get out there and exercise what rights you still have left. If that includes sitting in front of the American Embassy or whatever, then do that!'

Well, brevity never was his strong point. Billy added that he'd heard a lot of people saying that it was going to be a long hot summer, but he thought it was going to be 'a red angry summer' – and that was just in my flat.

Rachman was still hassling me through an onslaught of phone calls at work. I responded with a letter from the Legal Advice Centre. Mr Rachman sent my rent and deposit cheques back to me, announcing that he was refusing to cash them. He also claimed that although I had signed the contract, the landlord had not signed his section and therefore it was invalid.

Twenty years on, I still don't know why the landlord wanted me out. At the time, I thought it likely that the estate agents had made a mistake in letting the flat out again and the landlord wanted to sell it with vacant possession. Returning the cheques to Rachman, I sent him a further cheque for the next month's rent too.

Even then it struck me as surreal. Normally landlords threaten tenants for not paying the rent. I must have been the only tenant in Britain who was paying money to his landlord, who then insisted on returning it. Would I soon be sending my bailiffs round to Rachman's offices to force him to accept my hi-fi as well?

In addition to this, there was an ongoing argument about the deposit at Parsons Green. Lance, the landlord, was refusing to return my deposit in full, even though I knew Richard's girlfriend Sandie was ready to move in. He was incensed that I'd had the Fulham Legal Advice Centre send him a letter asking for my deposit and went into full Old Bill mode, wanting to arrange a 'meet' and accusing me of threatening to expose his sub-letting to the owners of the property (which I wasn't). It was an early lesson in property machinations. Everyone lies, everyone has something to hide and everyone is motivated by money. In the end, worn down by the travails at Fulham Broadway, I let him keep his £85. Property and greed – we all succumb to it.

Ronald and I busied ourselves trying to find a good drinking den around Fulham. We just wanted a friendly old man's pub rather than a boozer full of Sloane Rangers or a trendy bistro, but decent pubs were as hard to find in Fulham as landlords willing to accept your rent.

Mr Rachman made a personal visit to the flat and announced in his slippery fashion that if I did not leave, the landlord would take the law into his own hands and remove my possessions and change the locks on the door. I told him that I would only move if he could provide somewhere else that I was happy with for at least six months. My head was pulsating with the strain of it all. Apart from the permanent fear that I'd arrive home to find my stuff dumped on the Broadway, an additional worry was Ronald's dubious legal status. Was I allowed to have a sub-tenant? I had no idea.

THE SIEGE OF FULHAM BROADWAY

Mr Rachman then arrived in his BMW and drove me to a place in Ladbroke Grove. It was too small to accommodate Ronald as well so, not wishing to leave him homeless, I informed Rachman that it was not suitable. Back on Broadway, the landlord entered my flat with his own keys and threatened to throw all my things out, just as Mr Rachman had promised. I didn't even know his name – he was just the Sikh bloke who ran the shop downstairs – but I told him to get out and not to enter the premises without my permission. He cursed at me and left.

The following day, the increasingly desperate Mr Rachman showed me a place at Olympia which was OK and I said I'd take it. So that was it. Problem solved and my unhappy stay in Fulham over. Erm, no. Two days later, the increasingly schizophrenic Mr Rachman, who clearly belonged to the Arthur Daley school of business probity, announced that the Olympia move was off. Instead, he asked me to hide my stuff next Tuesday when the house was inspected by the landlord. It was as if we were in a Fulham Broadway farce. Rachman said the landlord knew I had an illegal sub-tenant. There was ominous talk of 'special conditions'. It was clear that I needed to see a proper solicitor, immediately.

It was not only the light fittings in the kitchen that were falling apart. My work was suffering. There was a misunderstanding at work on Friday, 13 July, the day a report on the health implications of dairy produce was published. I'd arrived at work early at nine o'clock, but the boss had announced that I should have been there at 8.30 to monitor the papers and that I should look for another job because I wasn't up to this one. I don't know if he meant it, but unemployment on top of homelessness was not that inviting a prospect.

I stayed at work for an hour, my hands shaking as I tried to drink a cup of tea from the tea lady at 10 a.m. Everything was closing in. I then walked out and retreated to my home that was not a home and lay on my bed looking at the walls. Later that afternoon, I took the District Line home to my parents' in Essex, a beaten and exhausted man. Whacked over the head with the property ladder, I was now suffering from non-executive stress. The next day I slept until 3 p.m., but at least my mother was there and I was in my old bedroom where no one was trying to evict me.

It was lucky that I had parents to retreat home to; without that option, it just takes a couple of bad breaks before you end up joining the homeless. After five days in Essex, I returned to Fulham having taken the week off work. Within two hours, the landlord was in the flat again. It was a campaign of sustained harassment designed to intimidate me into leaving. I'd always believed that in London it was villains who would try to enter your house, but it wasn't muggers and burglars who were attempting to break in to mine, it was estate agents and landlords. George Orwell had been a tad over-optimistic. Welcome to 1984.

One possible solution arrived when Heather, an old university friend who was now a nurse, said there was a room going at her new home in Camberwell. But after their appalling behaviour, why should I let Rachman and my landlord win by moving out? Should I stay or should I go? I resolved that my indecision would be final.

After another bad night's sleep, there was a visit to a lawyer in Hammersmith who charged £5 for a five-minute consultation that was of little use. A second lawyer, who specialised in housing issues, was much more helpful, advising, 'You could make money out this if you stand your ground, you could get enough for a deposit to put down on buying your own house!' It was symptomatic of the home-ownership mania that was sweeping the nation that the lawyer's first thought was that any payment for leaving could help me buy a flat.

That very evening, Ronald phoned to say the landlord had changed the locks and he had had to break in through the kitchen window, which, thankfully, proved to be less than secure. We then went for several stress-relieving pints in a local pub, leaving and returning through the kitchen window.

The next morning, my lawyer suggested that I could obtain an injunction against my landlord for £250. A phone call to Mr Rachman resulted in another offer. He said that if we left next weekend then the landlord would not charge me any rent for the two and a half months I had been living there.

Ronald and I had a long discussion. The place at Camberwell was in deepest south London but it was a fine old Georgian house and Heather had the lease for two years. Staying in Fulham might eventually result in an award of several thousand pounds but it could also result in a nervous breakdown. An older and stronger person might have stayed, but I opted to leave, save a couple of months' rent and maybe sleep at night again. Ronald said that he would stay with a friend for a few weeks and then look for a new place.

When I returned to work after a week's absence without leave, I wasn't shot, or even fired. The rest of the office appeared supportive, perhaps by then aware of the stress of my non-existent-home life. Three days later, Keith, who had rented the flat before me and was as bemused by the landlord's shenanigans as I was, came round in a white van to help shift my possessions to Camberwell.

It was a long voyage across the Thames to the mystical environs of south London, an area I had never explored properly before. As the Cottagers' fanzine said, there's only 'One F in Fulham' and I never wanted to see the place again. A lifetime's aversion to estate agents had commenced. All over the country, men in shiny suits like Mr Rachman were treating people like me with no respect and making huge sums of money in doing so. Camberwell beckoned and at last came the chance of solace from rogue landlords. Pete May was a man who had travelled a fridge too far.

MORTGAGE PROSPECTS: The applicant appears too intent on protecting his sanity to concentrate fully on the housing market. A protracted legal battle with his former landlord might have resulted in him obtaining enough money to put down a deposit for a new home, but he has opted for further renting. He does not appear to appreciate the value of a permanent, pensionable job. A sustained period of saving and a re-evaluation of his life's goals is advised if he is ever to gain a foothold on the bottom rung of the property ladder.

AVERAGE HOUSE PRICE IN GREATER LONDON: £48,379

6. The Camberwell Man

Camberwell Grove, Camberwell, London SE5
July 1984 to June 1986

My new house in Camberwell Grove was a palace. It was on the poshest road in Camberwell, lined with trees and elegant late-Georgian houses, built when Camberwell was still a village developing into a suburb. The politician Joseph Chamberlain was born at No. 188 in 1836. James Boswell had once visited his physician pal Ronald Coakley Lettsom here and Charles Dickens had described the tea gardens and ballroom at the Grove Chapel in *Sketches by Boz*.

For the first time in my life, I was living in a house with steps and columns outside the front door. The basement was let separately, but our house-sharing contingent had the rest of the building, including the use of both a front and back garden.

Inside the hallway, there was a chandelier and a huge circular staircase that would have suited Sebastian Flyte from *Brideshead Revisited* perfectly, shuffling his way downstairs, asking his mother if Jenkins had unlocked the cocktail cabinet yet. My room was huge with a double bed and an en suite bathroom. There were proper shelves for my books and hi-fi; no need for student bookcases of bricks and planks of wood. Even better, we had inherited a cleaner. There would be no arguments about house rotas ever again.

The house was owned by two doctors and was let for two years while they worked in America. Barring a Russian nuclear strike on

67

London, no one could attempt to evict me for 24 months.

Heather was an old friend from Lancaster University. Now working as a nurse, she was a socialist who liked both Billy Bragg and *EastEnders'* Dirty Den, so it was therefore a much more compatible mix than at Parsons Green. Two other nurses, sisters Paula and Caroline, were in the other rooms and we rubbed along fine.

The living room had two plush sofas and another chandelier. There was even something called a video. It was a huge great clunking thing with switches sticking out all over the place, making it look like a transmat machine from a Patrick Troughton-era episode of *Doctor Who*. Critics, and indeed The Buggles, were predicting that video would kill not only the radio star but also the cinema. It was indeed an amazing invention. We could go to a shop, take out a video of *The Terminator* and watch it at home. Even better, we could record our favourite TV programmes and if we weren't in, there was something called a timer that you set.

On *Top of the Pops*, The Smiths' singer Morrissey was confusing everyone by cavorting with a tree down his trousers and informing us that heaven knew he was miserable now. A youthful Bono, meanwhile, was giving boots and tight trousers a bad name singing 'Pride (In the Name of Love)' with U2. On Channel 4's *The Tube*, cool-for-cats Jools Holland and sex kitten Paula Yates were introducing the likes of Paul Weller's new soul combo The Style Council and Paul Young, who was singing the soulful 'Wherever I Lay My Hat (That's My Home)' – a sentiment I could empathise with. And we could record every moment of it!

The house contingent was completed a few weeks later when Ronald moved in. The fifth and final spot was an attic room on the third floor. Next to it was a door leading out onto a roof terrace with splendid views across the Grove's leafy gardens and over south London. Sitting on the roof gave us would-be Victorians a pleasing sensation of bourgeois elegance.

Ronald had been reluctant to move to Tubeless south London initially, but once he saw the house that was it. The clincher was the fact that his room had a fireplace (which was to prove a great aid to his seduction techniques). Soon he was burning bits of reclaimed timber, imagining that he was Alan Bates in *Women in Love* and fulfilling all his Lawrentian fantasies.

Of course, Camberwell also had its problems. We were close to dodgy Peckham and showers of glass by the pavement would indicate where the cars on our road had been broken into. During our stay, there was a murder when a geezer was shot in a pub on Camberwell Church Street in some sort of gangland feud. Camberwell Green was once a village green where Mendelssohn composed his *Spring Song*; it was now surrounded by traffic and a haven for drug addicts and super-strength-lager-drinking alcoholics.

The 184 and 176 buses had to negotiate an interminable queue of stationary traffic all along the Walworth Road before it was even possible to start a Tube journey at Elephant and Castle. It was just as difficult getting out from central London to Camberwell. Suddenly, no friends from north London would visit. The city was a bit like South Africa at that time – segregated by an ancient apartheid system. A Tubeless zone left most northerners quivering with so much fear that they could hardly hold their cocktails. But there was a real geographical Freemasonry among south Londoners: we would make our own entertainment with other south Londoners (if you try telling that to the kids of today they won't believe you).

You'd find yourself looking up people you hadn't spoken to for years simply because they had an SE postcode. Heather, Paula and Caroline worked at King's College Hospital and there were always plenty of nurses' parties going on. The nurses even had their own subsidised bar called the Penthouse within the hospital grounds. We had Camberwell College of Arts nearby too and lots of brightly plumed art students drinking at the Grove House Tavern. There was live music at the Half Moon in Herne Hill (where we saw an embryonic Housemartins after singer Paul Heaton had sent a handwritten letter to *Notes from Underground* telling us that they were quite good) and other pubs and clubs, such as the Fridge in Brixton.

RENT BOY

That house compensated for everything, even the 184 bus. The end of the summer of 1984 was glorious. South London had space and none of the pretensions of Fulham. My new home was too good to leave. With a book on my knee, I'd sit in the garden in a state of disbelief. Sunshine, grass, solitude, peace, no hassles, no Sloane Rangers, no traffic, no one trying to change my locks – I had forgotten what a decent home life was like after 14 months of rental health problems. Just watching the TV together was bonding. When flat-sharing is going well, you become part of a surrogate family.

Ronald and I had finally found a proper pub after our desperate search from the flat in Fulham. In Camberwell, there were several candidates to be assessed. Our house was close to the Phoenix and Firkin (situated above the British Rail station at Denmark Hill) which was popular with nurses and students and served lethal pints of Dogbolter ale. The Grove House Tavern had plenty of trendy art students, but even better was the George Canning. Halfway along Camberwell Grove was a delightful little alleyway which even contained an independent bookshop selling orange-spined Penguins and green-spined Virago books to the literati. The alleyway emerged on Dog Kennel Hill and there was the George Canning. It was a proper local with late night drinking and a prototype *Fast Show* character we used to call 'the man with three dogs'. Every night, he would drop in for a pint or two surrounded only by his three canine companions. When he started nodding at us when we came in, we knew we had made it as locals.

Ronald, Heather and I became regulars, frequently slipping in at half-nine or ten o'clock. At 11 p.m., there was normally a feeble attempt by the bar staff to make us drink up as U2's 'Pride (In the Name of Love)' or Frankie Goes To Hollywood's 'The Power of Love' blasted out of the jukebox. Invariably, we would be there until after 11.30.

While we were enjoying the George Canning, the rest of the country was still in turmoil. At the bottom of every Tube escalator, there were a couple of blokes in black polo-neck sweaters and donkey jackets covered in yellow 'Support the NUM' stickers, rattling collection buckets. Garden Gnome at work remarked that Arthur Scargill was worse than Hitler and they should let the miners starve. My old school mate Nick still lived in Bermondsey and was active in the Militant Tendency. He seemed to have a permanent contingent of miners billeted in his Bermondsey flat. You could tell they were miners because they were the only people in London with Freddie Mercury moustaches who weren't gay.

To add to the sense of conflict, the city was aware of the permanent threat of IRA bomb attacks. Every litter bin in Oxford Street was a potential suspect. In October 1984, the whole country was shocked when an IRA bomb in Brighton narrowly missed killing the entire Cabinet. It was reported that at least three people were killed, including one MP, and the incident provided the haunting image of an injured Norman Tebbit being carried out of the rubble in his pyjamas. Nobody I knew would admit to liking the Tories (and most of us thought that GLC leader Ken Livingstone was right when he said that the Government would eventually have to talk to the IRA), but trying to kill Thatcher and Co. was something else again.

Ronald and I responded to the bombs and pit-ballot disputes by getting drunk and reading J.P. Donleavy. Ronald had loved *The Ginger Man* and passed it on to me. As a validation of alcohol-fuelled debauchery, it was brilliant. For the next year, we became the 'Camberwell Men'. It was time to stop worrying about romance and just enjoy being dissolute. I realised that I had a good sense of humour and should use it. We invaded nurses' parties, social workers' parties, anywhere we could in pursuit of furtive canoodling and controversy.

While I was never as good at chasing women as Ronald, whose Celtic eyebrows and almost-working Morris Minor seemed irresistible to most of our female friends, my new Donleavy-esque persona had improved my romantic chances. Having a home worthy of the name helped, too. When no one is changing your locks, your chances of getting a drunken snog at a nurses' party increase tenfold.

Christmas arrived and 'Do They Know It's Christmas?' echoed

around the George Canning as drinking-up time expanded exponentially. Bob Geldof had gathered together all the top musicians of the day to record the number one single. The proceeds were going to help the victims of the horrendous famine in Ethiopia. At the time, I couldn't understand why he wasn't also speaking out against nuclear weapons and the closure of the pits, but back then I believed that a broad church was Westminster Abbey. Still, the aim of Band Aid was laudable – the tinted '80s barnets less so. Nik Kershaw and Howard Jones must still be very ashamed.

I spent New Year visiting my old West Kensington flatmate Julia in Edinburgh and becoming involved in a short-term long-distance relationship with her flatmate. But in the manner of Paul Young, London was where I was going to lay my hat and find my home.

My job at the National Dairy Council was merely a means of subsidising my social life and living in a great house. The journey to work was still interminable. Sitting on the bus trying to get to Elephant and Castle or even Oval Tube station during the morning rush hour was almost a religious experience, in that it gave the meditative mind a glimpse of eternity.

My job made no demands on me, but I knew that soon I would have to leave and try to write. I'd interviewed Billy Bragg for the latest edition of *Notes from Underground* and the fanzine was still my creative outlet. We were still selling it at Apples and Snakes gigs or other cabaret venues like the Albany Empire in Deptford. Inspired by the ranting poets, I'd even blagged a spot as the poetry editor of *Jamming* magazine (edited by Tony Fletcher and founded with money from Paul Weller), only for it to go bust within two months.

There had been rumours of redundancy at the NDC from the beginning of 1985. I consoled myself with thoughts of George Michael and Andrew Ridgley, that job or no job I am a man. Live Aid arrived in the summer of 1985 with everyone watching from our affluent piece of Camberwell. Elvis Costello caught the mood with an old Liverpool folk song called 'All You Need Is Love' while Bono posed in jodhpurs and memorably grabbed a girl from the audience to canoodle with during 'Bad'. It was a feel-worthy moment for the whole country.

A week later, I was feeling bad again, having been made redundant. I was middle class and certainly not starving – and anyway it was what I desired – but it still hurt. Some of the other workers at the Dairy Council were in tears. Many were too old to ever be employed again. Or they were the people who had taken out 100 per cent mortgages and were now wondering how they would ever repay them. The place was undoubtedly overstaffed, but it was the biscuits and coffee and platitudes beneath the flickering strip lights that were most upsetting. It would give me a chance to try and earn a living writing, but for the moment it had sent me clattering down the property ladder, head first.

At least there were six weeks left before we had to leave and a pay-off of two months' wages plus my pension money. My response to imminent unemployment was to put on my best red-check lumberjack shirt (for some reason they were fashionable at the time) and pogo to Billy Idol's 'White Wedding' at our house party. Heather insisted on 'Freedom' by Wham! being played again and again. Some of the guests were wearing Bruce Springsteen-style red bandanas around their heads. There were tousled big hairdos everywhere. It could easily have been mistaken for a Wham! lookalikes convention.

At one point, Ronald took a drunken walk in the back garden and fell into the basement, gashing his chin. He then had Heather and several other nurses standing over him in the kitchen, brandishing a kitchen knife and exclaiming 'Let's take him to casualty, great! It's brilliant on a Saturday night!' Even he wasn't drunk enough to accept.

Even a few north Londoners made it across the water. They were later left to wander the streets of the deep south, bemused by the lack of black cabs on Camberwell Grove. A mad Irish nurse was doing aerobics on the floor. Posy art students were wearing Bermuda shorts. Ronald's mate Bill was left asleep in a chair in the garden in the rain. Happy days.

Unemployment arrived in August and it was bliss not to

commute, shave or put on a tie, an accessory I've always hated. Life consisted of signing on and getting my rent paid legally through social security. The redundancy money from the NDC would help keep me solvent for a few months. Now was the time to travel, without any of that nonsense of having to ask the boss for permission.

I went to visit Julia and her new boyfriend again for a week during the Festival in Edinburgh, there was a week in Rome with Ronald visiting his sister and two weeks travelling alone around the Scottish Highlands in October. In Wick, a lorry driver in my hotel remarked that he could never live in London because he thought he would feel like a mole going underground all the time. What did he know? You could appreciate both the Duncansby Stacks and Elephant and Castle Tube station. After the peace of Skye, I appreciated Camberwell all the more.

The UB40 lifestyle was enjoyable after two and a half years of filing cuttings on milk, cream and cheese. It was a chance to listen to the new, much-slated Dexys Midnight Runners album *Don't Stand Me Down* – I thought it was a work of brilliance.

During the NDC's renovations earlier that year, I'd acquired my office desk for just £5 and used the company car to drive it to Camberwell. Now was the chance to use it for creative purposes. Free from unsatisfying work, I could write short stories and poetry in the style of Attila the Stockbroker, Seething Wells and Porky the Poet (later to be Phill Jupitus), and start sending some of my fanzine articles off to magazines.

The sunshine continued until well into the autumn and Ronald and I would sit on the roof terrace at dusk drinking cold beers and pretending to be gentlemen as we listened to the sound of petrol bombs going off in the Brixton riots. *Brideshead Revisited* was never quite like this.

A jolt to this lifestyle came in November when Ronald moved to a tower block in Westbourne Park. Some friends of his were members of a short-life housing association there and he could get his own flat for just £17 a week. These associations allowed the transitory population of London, people like myself, the opportunity to stay for a short period in a flat before the owners reclaimed them. Usually they were awaiting repairs, so the system allowed them to be occupied while they waited for the often tardy workmen to arrive. Ronald knew our lease was up the following summer and he had always been better at long-term house planning than me. He was also fed up with his Morris Minor being broken into by the kids from Peckham loitering on the Grove. The Camberwell Men were no more.

Thinking of the future, I applied to Southwark Council. Normally a single person with no children getting a council flat was as likely as Bob Geldof not having to contribute to his fookin' swear box while he fed the world. Yet within a few weeks, a flat on the North Peckham estate was being offered to me. The estate was notorious locally, but it was worth a look.

After several miles of rampways and corridors, I arrived at the flat. I felt a bit like Sigourney Weaver walking through that deserted spaceship in *Alien*. In Peckham, no one would have heard her scream; the place seemed deserted, bar the odd guard dog barking. Mind you, anywhere that was offered to a man with minus 200 housing points had to be dodgy. Moving to the North Peckham estate seemed like an invitation to be mugged, robbed or much worse. Be grateful for another six months in Camberwell Grove, I reasoned.

At the start of 1986 came a huge fillip. Paul phoned to tell me that my article on flat-sharing (do you get the idea of a theme here?) had been used in *Midweek*, one of the free magazines that was given away outside Tube stations all over London. It recounted my experiences with rogue landlords, withheld deposits, changed locks, rude notes and house rotas. It was fitting that my first-ever published feature was on renting. So far, it had been the passion of my life. My final feature was surely destined to be on flat-sharing, too, before I was buried with an epitaph reading: 'Rent Boy: If only he'd paid more attention to the house rota and got a proper job.' When I called *Midweek*, I discovered that I was going to be paid. Money for writing, this was incredible. It was to be the start of a long and ignoble career in journalism.

Inadvertently, and mainly through treating the DHSS as a wing of the Arts Council, I had discovered the life of a freelance journalist. NUJ classes on sub-editing and radio journalism and an evening course in freelance writing helped me move towards a new career as a hack.

Inspired by other fanzine writers, such as Richard Edwards of *Cool Notes*, I'd started going to Red Wedge meetings. Red Wedge was a loose alliance of musicians (Billy Bragg, Paul Weller, The Communards, etc.), artists and writers who were opposed to the Thatcher Government.

Amid a plethora of black polo-necked sweaters at places like the London College of Printing, I was rubbing DM shoes with Jerry Dammers and former *NME* editor Neil Spencer. A glossy magazine called *Well Red* with stylish design by the Fish Family was initiated and, although it was all unpaid, my articles and reviews were being published. Other young hopefuls included Essex lads and West Ham fans Phill Jupitus and big Joe Norris (who was later to manage a host of top comedians, including Phill).

Hell, I was even applying for jobs. After turning down the offer of a job writing for the British Sulphur Corporation Ltd (presumably I would have been a metal guru), I applied for a more suitable position advertised in *The Guardian* – that of editor's assistant at a magazine I shall call *London Life*, another free listings magazine. My *Midweek*, *Notes from Underground* and *Well Red* pieces were produced at the interview and, after doing a short subbing test, I was offered the job. By the middle of February, at the age of 26, I was working as a full-time journalist on a salary of £8,500 p.a.

London Life was in an overcrowded upstairs flat in Hammersmith and the first few weeks were exciting. You handed in your typed review (back then a VDU was something you hoped you wouldn't catch down the Wag Club) to the setting room and it came out typeset; then you'd watch as people with what looked like Airfix glue and cans of hairspray stuck your words on the final page proof.

It was incredible. I was being paid for writing reviews for singles, gigs, plays and restaurants, and interviewing the likes of Pete Townshend. I could sneak in articles on football at a time when suggesting that Chelsea would one day sign Italian, French, Nigerian and Liberian players would have earned you a DM boot wrapped round your head in the dilapidated Shed End.

My review of the Red Wedge concert at Hammersmith Odeon was in print. Margaret Thatcher wouldn't be able to stand this – pop stars subsuming their egos and all agreeing to play short sets. That evening seemed to sum up the mood of the early '80s; Tom Robinson performed an acoustic version of 'War Baby', one of the finest songs ever linking personal and political fears, while the sheer excitment of The Communards and Sarah Jane Morris performing the ebullient 'Don't Leave Me This Way' left everyone in the audience optimistic that the excesses of Thatcherism would soon be overturned. The Communards were even joined by Ken Livingstone on tambourine, who announced with some prescience: 'I've been abolished, but I won't go away!'

The only problem with *London Life* – and it was a quite a big problem – was my editor Darryl. She was scary: a 40-something woman from the arse-kicking old school of journalism. In a movie, she'd have been played by Glenn Close or Sigourney Weaver with shoulder pads the size of an American football player's.

Darryl could certainly spot talent and a number of her protégés went on to have fine journalistic careers, including one who edited *Time Out*. She would have been a fine editor for some types of journalist – but not for me. An introverted lefty Englishman who believed in constructive criticism was confronted with this brash über-editor who loved swearing and going to nightclubs and didn't like politics.

Another problem was that I had been hired as an editor's assistant. She essentially wanted a sub-editor and, while I was happy to do some subbing, I also wanted to write. And was an editor's assistant an assistant editor? We never did solve that one.

Darryl treated *London Life* as if it was of parallel importance to the *New York Times*. The office was noisy and uncomfortable, with cries of 'Who, what, why, when and fucking where!' being directed at various miscreants. Then there were terrible evenings at places like the Café des Artistes in Battersea, where conversations revolved around inner thoughts and Air signs.

In particular, Darryl would fire off hastily typed memos declaring that she was 'spitting nails' over an incorrect date on page 43 of this week's issue. One of her memos to me read: 'I know I've said your writing is good, but this weekend was the first time I've actually proofed and ingested any of it for a long, long time AND the bottom line is, YOU ARE STILL WORD WANKING and the stuff is much too verbose! Honestly, it's about bloody time you got your act together on brevity and sharp, tight, good writing!'

Darryl was the scourge of word wankers everywhere and, 18 years on, I still feel slightly guilty at continuing to make a career out of it.

Still, perhaps it was the only way to learn. To be fair to Darryl, initially I was struggling to keep up with the pace of producing a magazine each week. After *Dairy Mirror* at the NDC and then life on the dole, the relentless production schedules came as a shock. Particularly as the place was understaffed. But I'd soon adapted and felt that I was working hard and writing well and had much to offer the magazine.

One problem was that when confronted with Darryl's posterior-poking management style, I'd retreat into nervous silence. No doubt she thought that I was an over-earnest lefty who needed a bit of booting about the backside, but in my opinion it was certainly not effective man-management.

Full-time journalism was knackering, too. Camberwell Grove was a great place to live, but in commuting terms it could just as easily have been Brighton. There would be that tortuous bus ride to Elephant and Castle followed by a trip on the Bakerloo Line to Piccadilly Circus and then the Piccadilly Line to Hammersmith. Some days it was taking me 90 minutes each way.

But much had changed in 1986 and at least I had full-time employment. If I ever passed my probationary period, I'd be able to apply for a mortgage. That was a big if, however, because the magazine appeared to regard probationary periods as infinitely extendable. Way after three months had passed, I had no confirmation that I'd been officially employed nor received any statement of my terms and conditions of employment.

My accommodation was also on probation. In June, the two-year lease was up on our great old house in Camberwell. After looking at four places and glimpsing the pitiful world of occupied bathrooms in eight-person shared houses in Herne Hill, it was tempting to give up. Clearly, I needed to move nearer to the office, but exhaustion was upon me after long commutes and late nights out reviewing, all with Darryl ready to berate me in the morning for masturbating with words.

There was a horrendous nuclear accident at Chernobyl in the Soviet Union, with much alarmist talk about the reactor's nuclear core melting through its sarcophagus and heading towards the Earth's core. Radiation was drifting over Wales. Yet *London Life* seemed more concerned with nightclubs. As Chernobyl melted down, I felt I might soon be doing the same.

The world and Camberwell were ending simultaneously. My parents had by now moved to a modern three-bedroom house in Norfolk where you could still buy a house for under a hundred grand. My childhood home had gone and all my old copies of *TV21*, *Goal*, *Shoot*, *NME* and *Sounds* had been burnt. Even my parents, now in their late 50s, had managed to get on the property ladder.

Norfolk properties might have been cheaper than the rest of the South-east, but to succeed as a journalist I needed to remain in London. Word came that Julia, my old flatmate from Comeragh Road, was sharing with her friend Babs in Neasden and they had a boxroom to let. Knowing nothing of Neasden except that it was the subject of many a joke in *Private Eye*, I accepted. Julia and Babs were good people and it was close to the Tube and an easier commute to work.

Slowly, the occupants of Camberwell Grove drifted away. Meanwhile, more of my friends began to get married. Some of the guests at Paul and Katie's wedding took advantage of the empty house. After a hedonistic and eventful day as best man and an evening cruise on the *Marchioness* (tragically sunk after a collision with a dredger on the Thames in 1989), I retreated to Camberwell and awoke on the Sunday to see off the overnighters and sit in an empty home. There is nothing more desolate than a house bereft of its personal belongings. The other rooms were empty and my stuff was in boxes. Ronald soon came to move my stuff in his motor. The process took several journeys and lasted from 2 p.m. to 11 p.m. Camberwell to a boxroom in the suburbs. From Donleavy to redundancy and now itinerant journalism. Time to move that electric typewriter once more.

MORTGAGE PROSPECTS: The applicant delayed entering the property market for a further six months following redundancy. It is encouraging that he has now attained further employment but he needs to curtail all masturbatory activities with the English language in order to pass his trial period at *London Life* before he can be considered for a mortgage. Even if this happens, three times his income (£25,000) will be far too low to buy a one-bedroom flat in London. We suggest he finds a marriage partner or affluent companion willing to share a joint mortgage, or rich parents to help increase his equity.

AVERAGE HOUSE PRICE IN GREATER LONDON: £73,539

7. Sound of the Suburbs

Ballogie Avenue, Neasden, London NW10
June 1986 to Sept 1986

Neasden passed me by. It was the relationship you can't remember, the name in your diary that a few years later means nothing to you. Faced with the emotional trauma of leaving Camberwell, I simply went out every night and used my new house as a dormitory.

Ballogie Avenue was a road of identical 1930s houses with bay windows, glass alcoves around the porch and mock-Tudor beams around the upper storeys. It was a place where front gardens were converted into car parking places and stone cladding was thought stylish. You were greeted by a 'No Through Road' sign as you walked up Ballogie Avenue from the Tube and for me, at 26, it might as well have said 'No Life Here' as well. After the steps and pillars leading up to the majestic Georgian house, suburbia was stifling my rent boy's soul. It was soon apparent that this was another housing error. A few stations down the line, Kilburn was at least grimy-but-street credible. Here there were no buildings that were pre-1930s. I had surfaced in a soulless suburban sprawl.

At the end of Ballogie Avenue, the road terminated in an ugly grey wall that looked like it should have been at Checkpoint Charlie. It was about five feet high, but if you peered over it you would see the huge four-lane motorway of the A4088. Cars, buses and lorries sped past in a cacophonous convoy. This was Neasden's spaghetti junction. The truly uninspired could stand on their toes

81

watching traffic all day. An underpass and flyover held up the North Circular Road. It was like having the M1 at the bottom of our street instead of at Brent Cross.

Ten yards from where our road met the Berlin Wall, an ugly concrete pedestrian bridge rose over the A4088. It was only the width of two people and seemed to reverberate with every juggernaut that passed surely hundreds of feet below. It was advisable to check for border guards with rifles before venturing over the traffic flow. Walking to the middle of that precipitous edifice, it felt like you were about to be coerced into a quite possibly deadly bungee jump. Every trip to the shops necessitated this near-death experience. At least you could see the towers of Wembley Stadium from the top of the bridge. Another consolation was that it would be a handy area to live in should West Ham get to the FA Cup final before the end of the millennium (which they didn't).

Across the precarious pedestrian bridge, which even Harrison Ford would have balked at, was the heart of Neasden. The most unprepossessing broadway in the history of civilisation nestled at the rump end of Neasden Lane. The national chains had all decamped to Brent Cross. Despite the large Asian population, there was only one moribund curry house. It was just endless red plastic baskets outside hardware shops, Lloyds Bank, a sleepy post office, a somnolent baker, a bookies, a video shop, a fried chicken shop, two launderettes and a ghastly chain pub called the Outside Inn.

Even the few shoppers seemed almost apologetic for being there. The western end of the Broadway ended abruptly in the North Circular – you could stand by the railings and either admire the signs proudly advertising 'Neasden Subway' or watch the traffic race past at 60 mph. Forget London gridlock. Here every car was being driven in the fashion of the late Donald Campbell.

As for my new house in Ballogie Avenue, there was a spacious double sitting room, an adequate kitchen and a small back garden. It was rented through an estate agent and we seemed reasonably secure. It didn't cost too much. There was nothing wrong with it. But not much right either.

Julia and Babs both had decent-sized rooms but mine was tiny.

SOUND OF THE SUBURBS

There was a single bed and a white fitted wardrobe and only about two feet in between. My novel collection spilled precariously from the one available shelf while the rest of the books were piled on top of Babs' wardrobe next door. My old desk from the National Dairy Council, all metal edges and harsh contours, was deposited in the living room, along with my typewriter. I'd seem to end up there most Sundays writing copy and reviews for *London Life*. My hi-fi was there too, often used at night for reviewing singles as I pondered Billy Bragg's lyrics with Babs.

Julia and Babs were good flatmates. Julia had recruited me as an expert shopping-bag carrier during our Comeragh Road days; as organised as ever, she was now working for a travel agent. I'd been to visit her a couple of times when she was working in Scotland and we'd stayed close. After her spiritual sojourn in Celtic parts, she must have found Neasden as banal as I did. She knew her job was likely to keep her moving around the country though, so presumably she expected it to be only a temporary posting in suburbia.

Babs was a linguist who had met Julia at university and was now a Goth. Her hair veered between sensible work style and blonde cantilevered football stand. She spent her nights out clubbing to the sounds of the Sisters of Mercy and numerous other bands whose members had black hair and chiselled cheeks.

The real sound of the suburbs was pomp rockers. Occasionally, we'd hear the music from Queen concerts reverberating from the nearby Wembley Stadium – noise pollution in every sense of the word. Sometimes we'd walk to the Spotted Dog, a pub as bland as the rest of the area. Apart from that, Neasden had few hotspots, unless, of course, you counted a trip under the Neasden subway to the microwave meal section at Tesco.

But the undoubted attraction of Ballogie Avenue was that it was two streets away from the appropriately grey-coloured and dusty-looking Jubilee Line station. It took me much less time to reach work than from Camberwell, even if I did feel like Reggie Perrin, my morning walk taking in Ballogie Avenue, Lansdowne Road and Neasden Lane: 'Morning, Darryl, 13 minutes late, word wankers on the line at Dollis Hill!'

The station was a lifeline for my nocturnal sojourns. The Red Wedge crowd had introduced me to nights at Wendy May's Locomotion at the Town and Country Club in Kentish Town, where access was by black Levi 501s and polo neck only, and you might even see a couple of Housemartins. London offered gigs, parties, restaurants and football grounds to explore in my new role as a hack.

Theatre reviewing was not all glamour, though. Turning up to view a fringe play called *Curtains at the Rosemary Branch*, the audience consisted of a bloke from *Time Out* and me. It was as deserted as Neasden Broadway. Yet still the cast put on the play for us and it wasn't that bad either, so I gave them a good review. Besides, the cast wouldn't have had too much trouble remembering my face if I had slated them.

My work situation was as precarious as ever, though. I seemed to have passed my probationary period simply through not yet being sacked. I was working as hard as I could, improving as a sub-editor, writing well and putting in lots of unpaid weekend work, but Darryl's opinion of me seemed to fluctuate wildly. An article on CND caused more collateral damage than the entire Cold War. I'd omitted to mention that Bertrand Russell helped found the organisation. Even worse, Darryl then asked if CND vice-chairman Bruce Kent was some kind of religious nut. To an earnest lefty like myself, such a statement was as provocative as turning up with a Benny Hill video at an all-'wimmin' Greenham Common peace camp.

Further memos to editorial followed warnings that 'A team is only a set of components and components can easily be replaced.' I endured frequent discussions about me not fitting in.

Some days, this miserable word slave just didn't want to board the train to work. I looked on admiringly at the freelancers who came into the office to chat and hand in their copy. That seemed to be the way to go: judged by your words and ability, not the perceived defects of your personality.

Meanwhile, amid the mayhem of *London Life*, I was increasingly conscious of the booming property market. Alternative comedians like Ben Elton were joking about tossers at dinner parties discussing how much money they'd made on their properties. Ronald was still living in his Westbourne Park tower block for a very cheap rent, but like me could not afford to buy in London. He wanted to put his surplus income into property somehow, though, and asked me if I'd like to buy a house with him in Cornwall. They were going for under £30,000.

Ronald was a keen surfer and loved the area around Penzance. We'd visited before and it was a beautiful, spiritual spot, full of Neolithic monuments and ravaged cliffs. But Penzance was five and a half hours from London (about eight hours in Ronald's car, not allowing for his frequent breakdowns). Nor were Cornish fishing villages renowned for either their journalistic opportunities or welcoming attitudes to poncy London incomers.

A Cornish cottage might have worked as a holiday home, but really if I was ever to buy it had to be in London, where my work and writing potential lay. My desire to own a property was not so great that I would buy one at the other end of the country. In addition, buying with a friend could create problems when one person decided to move on. The most prudent use of my resources was to save what I could with the Abbey National and hope that one day someone would decide I was a media genius and throw large wads of tenners at me.

I thanked Ronald for his offer and pointed out the distance factor and the fact that my employment prospects at *London Life* were not exactly favourable. He bought a fine fisherman's cottage in Newlyn to use as a holiday home and to possibly move into one day. I was now the only living rent boy in London.

Ronald was still renting in Hermes Point as well and had some tantalising news about a possible flat going in his tower block as someone was moving out. Admittedly, it was full of asbestos, but it was apparently safe as long as you didn't disturb the walls. And amazingly it happened. Ronald's housing group decided to let me in. While most people thought of *Nine and a Half Weeks* as a film starring Mickey Rourke and Kim Basinger doing lewd things with ice, for me it was simply the time I'd spent in Neasden.

RENT BOY

My personal property ladder was still under a manhole cover somewhere on the Harrow Road, but here was hope of finally having my own rented place. Julia was likely to be moving on soon with her job and then there would be the familiar travails of finding a compatible tenant and some life in Neasden.

There's a great line in the film *The L-Shaped Room* which Ronald and I picked up on and would often repeat in the pub. The frustrated writer upstairs rants: 'I'm twenty-eight and what have I got, eight lousy short stories'. I was 27 and starting to feel similarly disillusioned. What had I got in my life apart from seven lousy flat-shares in homes that were not my own? Number eight would surely be the answer.

Solitude was what I desired. Asbestos be buggered. I gave my month's notice to the estate agent. It was that or jumping off the foot bridge over the A4088. After Neasden, I would have fallen out of bed at Chernobyl if I had been guaranteed my own flat.

MORTGAGE PROSPECTS: The applicant is at least aware of the interest in property prices at fashionable London dinner parties, but has declined an offer to step on the property ladder in Cornwall. He is working for a relatively low salary of £8,500 p.a. while under the threat of dismissal in a generally overheated property market and has now decided to become a downwardly mobile short-life council tenant in a tower block. We suggest the applicant urgently seeks a career reappraisal.

AVERAGE HOUSE PRICE IN GREATER LONDON: £73,539

8. Asbestos Rain Pissin' Down

2nd Floor, Hermes Point, Westbourne Park, London W9
September 1986 to May 1989

Hermes Point was a monolithic monstrosity of a 22-storey tower block that pierced the Westbourne Park sky. Next to it stood its bastard twin, Chantry Point. Both buildings had curiously rounded windows, reminiscent of the sort of thing you might see on a cross-channel ferry, or indeed a washing machine.

Kincardine Gardens, an apologetic three-storey box of flats with concrete balconies and flat roofs which encouraged permanent pools of rainwater to gather, nestled in between the two high-rise blocks. Even The Clash would have rejected Hermes Point as a possible album cover on the grounds that it was too gloomy.

The lifts in the block's foyer did little to improve the image. 'Asbestos rain pissin' down!' read the graffiti inside the malodorous tin box that could lift you up 22 storeys. It was a reference to my – quite possibly literal – status as a short-life licensee in an asbestos-clad monolith in the heart of toxic Westbourne Park. Still, at least the writer had put the apostrophe in the right place.

It was surely a mark of the desperation of the London housing market that no one considered the asbestos in the fabric of the blocks to be a problem. The flats were large and cheap and Westminster Council said that it was all quite harmless as long as we didn't knock nails or put screws into the walls. My London sojourn had taken in Turnpike Lane, West Kensington,

Hammersmith, Parsons Green, Fulham Broadway, Camberwell and sodding Neasden, and for the first time ever I had my own flat. All for £17 a week. The council was threatening to sell off the estates but that could take years. There was no way I would give this up.

Within the lifts, it seemed super-strength lager rain was also pissin' down. There must have been a man in London who made a living urinating in council-block lifts. Wherever you went, this ubiquitous character had been there before you. The two lifts were sarcophagus-like stainless-steel structures that smelt of both the aforementioned urine and Special Brew, a relatively new and lethal get-pissed-quick super-lager that was sold in blue cans, tasted like a combination of tequila and petrol and was the favoured tipple of the burgeoning underclass.

It was always interesting to peruse the graffiti inside the lift – if only to alleviate the perpetual anxiety that it might never make it to its selected destination or judder to a stop between floors. If this happened, you had to press an alarm button that looked as if it would summon help within, oh, the next decade at least.

Near the top of the lift someone had written, 'If you can piss this high, I will rate you.' Another person had used their felt-tip to daub 'Stick a fork in their arses turn 'em over they're done! From Knightsbridge to Johannesburg!' At least we had a better class of graffiti in Hermes Point.

Next to the lifts, there was a neglected (except on the numerous occasions the lifts broke down) set of stairs, covered in newly fashionable hip-hop tags, a daubed slogan of 'PIGS' and a pile of vomit. The foyer was a howling wind tunnel in winter. Its glass panes had long ago been smashed and replaced by scuffed plastic that was also soon kicked away. The whole edifice was covered in pigeon droppings. No one at the council seemed to have noticed that entry phones, secure doors or even a porter might have reduced the undesirables wandering in off the street and in the long-term saved them money.

At one side of the foyer, a stained steel container stood on rusting wheels, overflowing with black plastic bin liners full of decaying detritus. The tenants dropped their rubbish down chutes on the landings and the bags cascaded into this festering orifice. I was soon to discover that the cockroaches simply crawled up this rent in the heart of the tower block and said 'thank you very much for easy access to the flats'. CND was right about who would inherit the post-apocalyptic world: if cockroaches could survive the asbestos-ridden rubbish chutes of Hermes Point, then a nuclear war between America and Russia would surely be comparatively easy to negotiate.

Neasden it wasn't. Banal suburban living had been replaced by a land fit for cars and urban blight. Westbourne Park was dominated by tower blocks and the Westway motorway, otherwise known as the A40. Even the Tube station was curved, hugging the contours of the seemingly ever-present Westway. From the Hammersmith-bound platform you could see Trellick Tower. It looked like something from *Thunderbirds*: a grey monolith attached to a slightly thinner grey monolith by the sort of aerial corridors that I used to make with Lego when I was creating a futuristic city for battles between Mechanoids and Daleks. Trellick Tower had been built in the '60s by Erno Goldfinger and had spawned several smaller high-rise offspring, apparently marching alongside the Westway towards Paddington.

Turning left from the station, the visitor could enjoy a vista of the Westway arcing towards Royal Oak with six tower blocks in the distance, one of which I was informed was where Mick Jones of The Clash used to live. It was said that his mum still lived there. Ten years after punk, I imagined poor old Mrs Jones trying to get out to the shops, only to be confronted by yet another group of bondage-trouser-wearing Scandinavian punks wanting to know where the nearest white riot was.

Westbourne Park Road proceeded under the Westway and here a red-brick bus garage used the motorway as its roof. Perhaps it was an early attempt at integrated public transport. You wondered if at night teams of crack London Transport men abducted whole cars through a series of subterranean lifts and then brainwashed and trained their occupants how to be bus inspectors.

On the left was the Big Table bed company. This shop was

situated in an old station office and was an early enclave of gentrification. A glimpse through its windows revealed artisans in the shadow of the Westway forever sanding stripped pine beds and moving polythene-wrapped orthopaedic mattresses.

Beneath the Westway, the drone of the traffic above gave one the sensation of standing in the bowels of an aircraft carrier. By the Grand Union Canal stood Meanwhile Gardens where I'd once found myself at the Notting Hill Carnival. Although it wasn't very PC to admit it at the time, the Notting Hill Carnival had always struck me as one of London's most overrated attractions. Endless people did endless milling about. You milled about outside horrendously overcrowded Tube stations and you milled about down interminable streets looking for a can of Red Stripe.

On Carnival days, Meanwhile Gardens was full of people milling about, looking for their mates, trying to find a drink and half-listening to a reggae outfit. But now it was empty, its tundra-like grass trailing away to the banks of the canal which, throughout my four years in the area, contained a half-submerged shopping trolley resting in black water. It's one of the mysteries of urban life why people shop at supermarkets and then dump their trolley in local waterways, but there must be whole species of fish and vegetation specially adapted to living with them.

On a bridge over the Grand Union Canal stood the pub that was to become my local: the Carlton. The main bar was upstairs, but its basement had canalside tables and chairs and stunning views of the odd rat and solitary barge.

Harrow Road met Westbourne Park Road in a dingy crossroads. There were several dodgy-looking pubs, a 7-Eleven on the corner providing unappetising fodder at all hours, a few apologetic burger bars, a baker and a gents' outfitters that looked like it had been there since the 1950s.

A hundred yards along the Harrow Road, appropriately positioned opposite Harrow Road police station, was my new gaff at Hermes Point. My flat was on the second floor. This made it easy to enjoy the credibility of tower block living without suffering vertigo. I always thought that Hermes Point would make a great name for a character in a novel. Hermes was the Greek messenger of the gods who showed the souls of the dead to the land of Hades – which was presumably a bit further down the Harrow Road somewhere towards Willesden.

Naming tower blocks after Greek gods could only have happened in the early '70s. It's doubtful if many of the denizens of the Harrow Road were that familiar with Greek mythology, so perhaps whoever named the block just had a sense of humour. Hermes was also the god of thieves and commerce, which in view of some of the dealings going on in the stairwells seemed strangely apt.

Having previously visited Ronald in his seventh-floor flat, I was already familiar with the grim environs that greeted the visitor to Hermes Point. But the defects of the communal areas were made up for by my flat. Compared to the private sector, these places were huge. I was used to one room and a corner of the sofa if I was lucky, with someone always there to complain about the washing-up not being done.

Some of my more ecologically aware lefty companions had drifted off to places like South America in search of pure wilderness, but here was all the space anyone could ever need. This was pure wilderness to me. Acres of living room, hectares of bog and some previously undiscovered wildlife in the kitchen (which I later identified as the indigenous Westbourne Park cockroach). Here, I could loll in my dressing gown all day, refuse to wash up or clean, play Elvis Costello's *Blood and Chocolate* at unacceptably high volume, shout at the TV when West Ham had lost and no one would judge me.

Then there was the rent. It was just £17 a week, which was nothing. This was the cheapest accommodation I had ever found in London bar squatting. We were part of a housing association, which Ronald and myself referred to as 'the Group'. The Group's seven flats were held by a civil-service trade union turned short-life housing association. Matthew, the leader of our Group, whom I knew vaguely from my days at Lancaster University, was the only one of us who was a civil servant. One of the Group had moved out, and now, thanks to Ronald's influence, I was in.

RENT BOY

The reason the council was renting the flats to us short-lifers was the uncertainty over the asbestos in the walls and beams. But at least it was safely contained for the present. And it was unlikely we'd be burnt in our beds in the event of a fire. Asbestos? I could handle it.

My splendid new gaff consisted of one big bedroom, a spacious living room, a kitchen, a bathroom and a large corridor worthy of *Doctor Who*. It even had airing cupboards and unlimited warm air (and asbestos fibres, we learned later) billowing from vents in the walls. The bad-taste brown wallpaper of a previous tenant was beautifully offset by Ronald's push-bike and VW Beetle exhaust. My flat soon became his unofficial annexe, as most of the space in his flat was taken up by three ancient baths, which he had discovered outside houses that were being done up. He reasoned they were too much of a bargain to ignore and that one day, when he had his own place, he might install them. We had to tread lightly over Ronald's baths, for we were treading on his dreams.

The flat was empty when I moved in, just shiny black tiles on the floor, those launderette windows and mounds of dust. Slowly, I attempted to furnish the place and follow the advice of my style guru, Vicky at *Ms London*, who said paint everything white.

In a furtive foray into what was then known as yuppiedom, I bought a £100 stripped-pine double bed base and mattress from the Big Table bed company by Westbourne Park Tube. The rest of the furnishings were the result of skip-diving, kerbside recycling and begging. The Maida Vale environs attracted a better class of rubbish. Some pieces of blue office carpet found in a nearby skip very nearly fitted the floor space in my bedroom. A 1960s revolving armchair covered with brown plastic was with some difficulty wheeled home from a skip in Notting Hill.

My dressing table was liberated from a doomed Chiswick squat inhabited by an Aussie member of staff at *London Life*. My wardrobe was a dodgy MFI creation with collapsing rails and detachable hardboard back, donated by Paul and Katie, who also presented me with their old cooker and a discarded black, very wobbly Habitat unit for my hi-fi when they moved from Notting Hill to Barnes. (By now, they had mastered the art of trading up in the property market – unlike myself.)

The TV cost £10 from another member of the Group. It was perfect apart from the fact that it took 15 minutes to warm up and made every presenter look shorter and fatter to the point where I thought Les Dawson was omnipresent on all channels. Even Lofty from *EastEnders* looked unfeasibly wide when he was jilted by Michelle. My new television also had a liking for lurid Technicolor, so that Dirty Den's face frequently resembled a flamboyantly created pizza.

Self-declared 'style guru' Robert Elms had just been interviewed for the *Sunday Times'* 'A Room of My Own' feature, boasting about his room with a designer crack on one wall. There would be no designer cracks on my walls, just credible furniture from the street. And, of course, very few women would be able to resist my love shack in W9, resplendent with pristine pine bed and carpet from a skip; I sensed it would be some time before it was featured in the *Sunday Times* or *The World of Interiors*.

Hermes Point was my first experience of life on a council estate. Initially, I had the odd twinge about urban deprivation and the Elgin estate resembling something from *Blade Runner*. But soon it became evident why the graffiti in the lift was more eloquent than the usual obscenities on council estates – some 80 per cent of the flats were inhabited by bohemian short-life licensees and the atmosphere was as close to 1930s Paris as you're ever likely to get. No wonder they knew where to place apostrophes. I had never lived anywhere more middle class.

Social workers, journalists, musicians, actuaries, students, sculptors, people called Piers and resting actresses and playwrights were to be found in virtually every flat. It was likely that Ernest Hemingway and Henry Miller were holed up there somewhere too. Because, although housing associations are meant to be for the poor, it's only ever the middle classes who have the qualifications to cope with the endless form-filling, the committees and the regular meetings. Only the middle classes could ever feign excitement at being elected deputy chair of the membership applications sub-committee.

In the outside world, both house prices and rents were continuing to rise. The Group spoke of little else. Most of the Group were decent people who, like myself, had just been beaten up a bit by life and flat-sharing. But, boy, could they do misery. After a few weeks of tower-block living and drinking with the Group in the Carlton, it became apparent that they were the most pessimistic group of people I had ever met.

Some of them were as old as 30-plus, which, to a 27 year old like myself, marked them down as almost Jurassic. Most of the Group had broken up from long-term relationships. It was an enclave of determinedly single people who would scurry from floor to floor throughout the Points drinking real coffee in their council flats.

Members would occasionally seduce each other or some hapless musician who happened to pass by, but they were mainly commitment phobic. It brought a new meaning to the term group sex. I was beginning to understand interbreeding within the upper classes and populations on isolated islands. Marooned in our tower blocks, feasting only on bitter at the Carlton, we were practically our own indigenous species.

Once, I made the mistake of asking a member of the Group for a second date. As we listened to a Joni Mitchell album, the woman involved simply replied, 'How many happy couples do you know?' I think that meant no.

It wasn't so much the statement which was shocking as her utter certainty that I wouldn't be able to contradict it. For her, relationships had as much chance of success as Neil Kinnock had of transforming Labour into an electable socialist government. (I, of course, knew that her Kinnock doubts were ridiculous and that his radical, soon-to-be-elected Labour government would dump nuclear weapons, transform the economy, restore social cohesion and maybe even give us affordable flats overlooking the parliamentary road to socialism.)

As Group members, we lost ourselves in copious drinking and discussed the free-market rental sector as if it were some Inuit region in the far north of Greenland. 'Do you know what it's like out there? They're charging £100 a week for a one-bedroom flat!' someone would say in awed tones. We'd then all console ourselves that downwardly mobile asbestos-ridden poverty at a rent of just £17 a week was the only option available to us bar another pint.

Three months after moving into Hermes Point, I lost my ticket onto the property ladder completely: on 21 November 1986, I was sacked from my job at *London Life*.

In a way it was a relief. Waiting at Westbourne Park station each morning to catch the Tube five stations westwards towards Hammersmith, I knew that I didn't want to arrive. When I was on board, I wanted it to be twenty stops, not three. My passion to write had been drained. Kevin Rowland wouldn't have tolerated it, Billy Bragg would have decided there was power in a union (only we didn't have one) and Elvis Costello would simply have produced another bile-induced album. Only this wasn't music, this was my life.

Four weeks earlier, Darryl had unexpectedly ushered me into a side room and told me that she was putting me on a month's 'trial', which, having worked at the place for nine months already, seemed completely ridiculous. The magazine was experiencing financial problems and no doubt there was pressure to cut costs. Even so, I was having more trials than Kafka's Josef K.

On the day of my dismissal, I'd drunk several beers while interviewing Lee Brilleaux of Dr Feelgood in a pub outside Euston station. It would be a good piece, yet I knew it was unlikely ever to be printed. When I returned to the office, Darryl handed me a typed letter in an envelope. For once, she wasn't talkative. It ended by terminating my employment and attached were copies of several warning memos. And yes, there was the 'word wanking' diatribe.

It was almost funny. Even at the time I'd thought that word wanking might have proved somewhat messy with all those page proofs and manual typewriters about. And surely it must have contravened health and safety regulations within those sweaty, overpopulated offices.

My chest tightened. I resolved that I would handle this with stoicism and an utterly phlegmatic response – so I walked right out of that infernal office never to return to *London Life* again. At home, seething inside, I poured myself a whisky, sat at my typewriter and wrote a resignation letter to *London Life*. It disputed all the allegations in my letter of dismissal and announced that I had no intention of working out my notice. Copies were also sent to the directors of the company.

That night, I joined Ronald and Jane from the Group in the Carlton. Ronald was bemoaning the fact that he'd just split up with one of his two on–off girlfriends. He was now adapting to serial monogamy through being indecisive about two women. He would go out with one of them for several months before changing his mind and going out with the other: to a man with no job or girlfriend, it didn't sound like too big a problem.

Jane had broken her ribs horse riding and I had been sacked. As we morosely tackled our pints and my pessimism quotient became stuck on red, it felt in some strange way like I had finally been accepted by the Group. I was 27, unemployed and as miserable as they were.

In many ways, the job had been useful. I'd had 28 features published, learnt to sub-edit, interviewed people like Billy Bragg and the Housemartins, and reviewed gigs and plays all over London. Only now my CV wasn't looking too great. Redundancy had been followed by dismissal.

For months, I'd wanted to leave and go freelance. My £17-a-week flat might just save my career. Having been sacked for alleged incompetence, it was doubtful if any other magazines would employ me. If I'd had a mortgage, my home would have been repossessed in a few months and I'd have been sleeping under the Westway, drinking Special Brew. Yet here in Hermes Point I could lie low waiting for the big one (again).

For a few days, it was bliss to sleep in and not travel down the Metropolitan Line. After a miserable, dissolute Christmas, my housing benefit finally arrived (for some reason no one seemed to worry that I'd been sacked and they just paid it anyway) and I signed up for the Enterprise Allowance Scheme. Let's give Maggie some credit: this was one of the best things the Thatcher

Government ever did. If you became self-employed instead of signing on, you were paid £40 a week for a year and could keep whatever else you earned on top.

My dad was still as pessimistic about the housing market as ever and I did wonder if he had been a member of the Group in his younger days. What was he talking about? It was obvious that prices had gone up ever since the war and would continue going up.

My father was the only person who advised me to fight back over my dismissal. After a visit to the Citizens Advice Bureau, I opted to go to an industrial tribunal over *London Life* issuing an untrue statement of dismissal, even if everyone else said that it was madness to pursue such a claim. The most I could win would be a retraction of the reasons given for my dismissal and two weeks' wages, but I was rather looking forward to using the phrase 'word wanking' in a legal setting. The Advisory, Conciliation and Arbitration Service (ACAS) became involved and a lengthy mediation process between *London Life* and myself ensued.

Halfway through these negotiations, it emerged that Darryl had also departed from *London Life*. With a new editor in charge, a settlement became more likely. It was a huge fillip to my faltering confidence when two weeks' wages duly arrived along with a new reference admitting that I could both write features and sub-edit.

At the start of March 1987, my enterprise allowance payments began. I was joining the tower block's other trustafarians and bohemians in our asbestos-ridden hive of low-rent, high-quality artistic endeavour. Amid the numerous people in my tower block claiming enterprise allowance in order to follow a career as a freelance sculptor or musician, I was perhaps unique in that I did eventually start to earn some money.

Slowly, my flat in Hermes Point became the home to successful freelance activity. As a sign of my professionalism, I had even purchased a device known as an answerphone, which would allow me to receive messages while I was out. I could record bits of music like the theme of *Doctor Who*, *Thunderbirds* or *The Prisoner* on my outgoing message. It was such a novelty that some people would ring me up just to listen to it.

Dismissal by *London Life* had kick-started my career. At the time, I was full of bitterness, but if I met Darryl today, I'd shake her hand. Proving her wrong gave me the determination to succeed as a freelance journalist. There was still my unpaid work for *Well Red*, the Red Wedge magazine, and Bill Williamson at *Midweek* began to publish my work. He could even commission features without shouting at me. There was work as a sub-editor on *Midweek*, too. The lads in the office liked long lunches, everyone had a pleasing anarchic sense of humour, the writers had real talent and it was all far more relaxed than my days at *London Life*. When, on my first day subbing, a new member of editorial spent all afternoon slumped drunkenly over his desk, before gatecrashing a birthday drinks session and then being publicly sacked, I thought, this is my kind of magazine. No wonder *Midweek* had Jeffrey Bernard as a columnist.

Through a contact in the Group, I was commissioned to write some pieces for *ROOF*, Shelter's housing magazine. And it was a source of huge pride when my first news piece made it into *City Limits* (never mind the fact that they paid you about two pence). At last, I had infiltrated a credible lefty magazine that would be read by right-on women with dangly earrings who lived in Stoke Newington. As Arthur Daley put it, 'the world was my lobster'.

That first *City Limits* piece was all about Westminster Council's attempts to sell off the 250 homes on my estate. Unemployment had given me the time to study the case in detail. Westminster Council, in the country's richest borough, was in many ways the Thatcher Government in microcosm. Its leader, Lady Shirley Porter, certainly shared the Iron Lady's compassion for the dispossessed.

Westminster Council had decided that it was going to sell off the Walterton and Elgin estates to private developers. There had been no consultation with the residents about this. They planned the sell-off despite the fact that there were 9,000 registered homeless people, including 538 homeless families, in the borough. Westminster Council had 1,500 empty homes boarded up with steel doors, each costing the rate payers £50 a week, or a total of £75,000 a week.

The model for privatisation could be seen at the Falcons in

Wandsworth, the other Tory flagship borough. The name was revealing enough. *Dallas* meets Jackie Collins. This former council tower block was surrounded by a high brick fence – to keep out the dispossessed – and flanked by an imposing gateway and ridiculously nouveau riche ornamental falcons. There was a new glass frontage around the foyer, a concierge and entry phones. All the things that were never even considered for council tenants.

The Walterton and Elgin Action Group (WEAG) had been formed to fight the sell-off and took the unusual step of bussing real-life tenants to developers' offices and housing committee meetings. It was run by a man called Jonathan Rosenberg. He'd moved to the estate in 1979 and over the years did a tremendous job of fighting the council.

Unlike the Elgin estate with its short-lifers, the Walterton estate was full of real council tenants, many of whom had lived there nearly all their lives. The sell-off was being opposed by 90 per cent of them, as well as us short-life licensees. Courtesy of Dante Developments plc, we would have no right to re-housing and would be back in the maelstrom of looking through the *Standard*'s flat-share column.

The atmosphere of near-war with the council could be gleaned from the Sitex steel doors that the council used to board up empty flats on the estates. Once they were sealed, the flats would lie empty, awaiting sale to anyone who lived or worked in the borough. WEAG had neatly stencilled 'This door costs you £50 a week. TORY WASTE' on a number of these. Other posters featured a clawed digger inside a bowler hat and suit and the slogan 'We are a little worried about our landlord'.

Those Sitex doors were all part of Westminster's policy of creating 'stable communities'. These stable communities did not refer to the Second Coming, but communities full of Conservative voters. Strangely, many of the council homes being sold off seemed to be in marginal wards. The homeless families fared little better. Westminster was seriously arguing that it should be able to deport its homeless to pre-fabs in areas like Barking and Hounslow.

My first housing committee meeting at City Hall was an

extraordinary shock. While Lady Porter made Margaret Thatcher look like a wet, her councillors were to individual thought what Michael Heseltine was to self-effacement. The Tory councillors would arrive in shiny new suits, able to fit their council commitments around their hours of business. The Labour councillors would arrive knackered after a full day at the office.

At one point, the chair of housing gave the protesters one minute to put forward their case. One Labour councillor shouted 'You're talking about people's homes, you ignorant pig!' A petition of 1,100 residents against the sell-off was unrolled in the chamber. It was immediately taken away – to prevent it being damaged – provoking cries of 'out of sight out of mind!'

'This is better than watching *Dallas*!' mused a fellow short-life protester.

What was striking was how scared these elected politicians were of the public. It all turned into something like a scene from a Tom Sharpe novel when the chair of housing left the 17th floor of City Hall and tried to reconvene the meeting on the 14th floor, without several of the Labour councillors. Those in the public gallery followed, along with several TV crews and radio reporters, pushing their way into a tiny overcrowded committee room. A few old ladies started singing 'We shall not be moved'.

The Conservative councillors decided there was disorder and called the police. The police arrived, somewhat baffled by the situation, and ruled that it was not an offence for the public to attend a public council meeting. 'You can run, but you can't hide!' declared councillor Neale Coleman, Labour's master of appropriate clichés. The Tories voted through their proposal to sell off the estate anyway. Such was my introduction to local government.

At a special meeting of the policy and resources committee, called to discuss the 'disorder' at the previous housing committee meeting, Lady Porter announced that the 60 WEAG members in the audience must 'listen in silence'. A Conservative councillor then called the protesters a 'ragbag of extremists', causing uproar in the gallery.

What was genuinely shocking was the contempt the councillors had for the decent, long-serving council tenants. The police were called again. 'I fought six years in the war for this – a police state!' shouted one irate 83-year-old pensioner called William Rae, standing on a chair. Lady Porter claimed that a councillor had been threatened. Mr Rae identified himself as the alleged assailant. After some deliberation, the Conservative councillor explained that his remark was directed at the Labour Group, not the residents.

When the meeting was reconvened, the council voted to ban all photography, video cameras and banners from future meetings, to eject members of the public who were not 'quiet' and to name Labour councillors judged by the chair to be contributing to the 'disorder'. Such was the state of open democracy in Westminster.

The company that was to buy the estates would be paid £1 million to take them over and then stood to make a profit of around £6 million once all the flats were sold: each one estimated to sell for around £87,000. Even those tenants who had taken up the right to buy would be evicted in order to give the new owners vacant possession.

The market for the redeveloped flats would be yuppies, complained the horrified tenants. The term yuppie had been enthusiastically adopted by the media to describe 'young upwardly mobile professionals'. Yuppies wore large glasses like Brains from *Thunderbirds* and carried bulging Filofaxes filled with useless information. The worst of them even carried huge devices that resembled small briefcases which they held to their ears while shouting things like 'Buy! Buy! Buy!' and 'Ciao!' Of course, we all knew that these boxes with huge aerials sticking out, known to the initiated as mobile phones, were a ridiculous fad and would clearly never become popular apart from with a few over-salaried prats.

WEAG's response to the council sell-off was both brilliant and amusing. A coach full of residents and journalists arrived unannounced at the offices of one of the potential developers and we told the flustered receptionist that we'd like to be consulted about our homes being sold. Then Rory McLeod, a folk singer who lived in Hermes Point, took out his acoustic guitar and led the throng in a chorus of WEAG's anthem 'Defending Our Homes'.

RENT BOY

Men in suits ran around like harried termites pursued by anteaters, bemused to find a mini-Glastonbury festival breaking out in their sanitised yuppie offices. Comedian Mark Thomas made a living out of this sort of thing years later, but at the time it was a highly original and effective tactic. 'We wanted them to know what it feels like to have your space invaded,' Jonathan Rosenberg explained to the video cameras.

Another full council meeting debated Westminster's brilliant idea of privatising three cemeteries and selling them off for just 5p each, 15p the lot. One of the gatehouses alone was later sold off for £175,000 by the private companies. By the summer of 1988, some estimates valued the cemeteries at around £5 million.

What was striking was the automaton-like nature of Lady Porter's councillors. When faced with protesting relatives of the dead, distraught that the graves of their parents and children had become overgrown and vandalised since privatisation, not one of the councillors could look to their conscience, think as an individual and vote for an independent inquiry into the sale of the cemeteries. There was something deeply rotten about this so-called 'flagship' council.

While life as a housing agitator was both exciting and giving me material for articles, my romantic life suddenly improved too. There were hot dates with Siobhan, a musician I'd encountered at Red Wedge meetings. My success must surely have been due to that new black polo-neck jumper I'd bought, which, along with my Dr. Martens shoes, a Fred Perry polo shirt and a Levi's jacket, was an essential accoutrement for any lefty in the late 1980s.

At 22, Siobhan was full of enthusiasm for life and a myriad of other projects, and any woman who could laugh all the way through *Star Trek: The Voyage Home* had to be love material, I reasoned. She was so attractive, I could hardly keep my eyes off her mortgage repayments.

She lived in a flat in Hammersmith which had been bought for her by her parents. As we breakfasted on honey on toast and freshly squeezed orange juice in long-stemmed glasses, listening to U2's *The Joshua Tree*, the spring sun illuminating her living room, I couldn't suppress my feelings of real-estate envy.

ASBESTOS RAIN PISSIN' DOWN

'The flat's an investment for my mum and dad,' she'd point out, which is what everyone who'd had a flat bought for them by their parents always said. Her dad had little hesitation paying £2,000 to buy her a new Roland keyboard on which she'd sing Madonna's 'True Blue' and other covers by the material girl, I noted.

Siobhan had to pay the mortgage on her flat herself, but even so, as I struggled in my short-life flat under threat of eviction or privatisation by Lady Porter, I couldn't help but reflect on what a massive advantage it was to gain a foothold on the sacred property ladder so easily. She would never have to worry about accommodation in London again. How different my own life might have been if I'd had that security. But still, at least all this short-life living was putting asbestos fibres on my chest.

While I was seeing Siobhan, Margaret Thatcher won the 1987 election. On the day of the Conservative victory, U2 played a brilliant gig at Wembley and I watched Bono adapt a line from 'Bullet the Blue Sky' to 'and run into the arms of Margaret Thatcher'. Ronald had by now bought his cottage in Cornwall, which I was free to borrow, and the next day Siobhan and I retreated for five days to a world where politics didn't seem to matter so much.

Siobhan's moods varied as much as my housing prospects, though, and despite being in the Labour Party she seemed to have some pretty suspect values. When an opportunity to sing in Dubai came along, Siobhan decided that she must, like Madonna, pursue her career. She flew away in the summer of '87, met a Texan with a BMW and I never saw her again.

This was all profoundly depressing, but the Group proved supportive. Peter Gabriel and Kate Bush were intoning 'Don't Give Up' across the airwaves. I found myself sharing endless cups of real coffee in council flats with various Group members and bemoaning the frailties and delusions of relationships. The more nihilistic I became, the more they seemed to like me.

A trip to a Billy Bragg concert with Clara, an old friend of Paul and Katie's who now lived a few streets away, helped. She had a high-octane personality, veering between the extremes of

Christianity and utter hedonism. We dated on and off for a few months and spent many hours trying to decipher the lyrics of U2's 'The Unforgettable Fire', before she finally moved back to Cheltenham. Though Clara did leave a lasting impression on my life – she donated her landlord's bad-taste brown-checked extremely non-flame retardant sofa, which was to feature in my living rooms over the next eight years.

Soon it seemed that I had scored again. There were a few hardy council tenants who had been in the tower blocks since they were built in 1971. They were either very committed, very conservative or very mad, as in the case of my neighbour, a large West Indian woman whose six children had grown up, leaving her alone and evidently a couple of sheep short in the top paddock.

I knew something was wrong when a pair of voluminous pink knickers came through my letterbox. They smelt of pungent, cheap perfume and, despite my expanding girth from drinking real ale in the Carlton, would never have fitted me.

The flats survived the Great Storm of 1987, which ripped down trees in Kew Gardens and caused mayhem all over the country, and on the eighth floor, Ronald was a little disturbed to see the water in his loo moving from side to side. Only I was encountering something far more dangerous than a mere hurricane. By late October, my noisy neighbour was becoming violent. One night, just after midnight, I heard the sound of breaking glass. Not someone trashing the landing windows this time, it was actually in my flat. A vase had come crashing through the bathroom window, thrown by my mad neighbour.

This was a first. Even mad Kirsty hadn't thrown objects through my windows. Unlike Nick Lowe, I did not love the sound of breaking glass. After a call to the Old Bill, a friendly policewoman arrived half an hour later and suggested that I contact social services rather than have my neighbour prosecuted. 'You won't be needing these, will you?' she asked, gingerly picking up the offending outsize ladies' pants. I showed her to the door, somewhat embarrassed by my new knicker-garnering persona.

Another morning, at around 6 a.m., I heard a gruff voice outside shouting 'Open up or we'll break the door down!' Ah, the community police, I thought. My neighbour's door came crashing down. The six young officers, searching for drugs allegedly connected with one of her sons, didn't know what they were tackling. A riot of abuse followed before my neighbour imperiously swept through the shards of splinters around her broken door and left carrying her shopping bag.

Then came the notes. 'I need a friend and companion. I need someone to do odd jobs for me and protect me during the night,' they read. She started to peer through my letterbox just as deadlines loomed. Once I opened the door and she rushed past me, deposited herself on the sofa and started telling me the story of her life. It looked like I had finally pulled.

On another occasion, I found her on the landing with a tin of red paint, writing 'My husband is a wanker' in three-foot-high letters on the wall. I suppose it was her version of a community mural. Hot meals would suddenly appear in casserole dishes on my doorstep. Then a plastic rose. My parents came to visit me and she began to push shards of broken glass through my letterbox.

I photocopied her copious correspondence and sent it to social services, before phoning her doctor and getting him to agree to visit her at home. There was even a visit from the real community policeman.

'I have noticed there are always tears in your eyes and at times I do wonder what is the matter with you,' read another note, at which point tears did indeed start to fill my eyes. This woman would have been enough to reduce her good Lord to a weeping wreck. When I finally escaped for a holiday in Greece, she attempted to follow me to Heathrow and I found myself ducking and running through the side streets of Westbourne Park desperately trying to lose my new friend.

Then one day she was gone, presumably either re-housed or certified. My new neighbour was a Sitex steel door, marginally saner and less prone to sending me knickers and notes.

Experiencing an unaccustomed inner peace, I looked at one of her notes again. 'In the Lord I take refuge,' it read. At times, I had been tempted to do this myself. Her note continued: 'Upon the wicked He shall rain snow, water, fire and brimstone'. And quite possibly vases and asbestos dust too.

Another year and a half of short-life living, drinking and eviction threats followed. For all its drawbacks, Hermes Point was home. Even the cockroaches didn't seem that bad. Every few months, there would be an infestation and a man from the council's pest control department would arrive looking like he was about to take one giant leap for mankind. Clad in a gas mask with a canister on his back, he would spray chemicals around the cupboards and walls and then tell me to keep my windows open for the next day, before floating off to rendezvous with Buzz Aldrin. The cocktail of asbestos fibres and pesticides in my flat could probably have helped the Americans win the Vietnam War.

The country was in the middle of an obscene property boom. Earlier that year, in February 1988, a converted broom cupboard opposite Harrods in Knightsbridge was sold for £36,500. It was five feet six inches wide and eleven feet long, with no cooker. Even I wouldn't live in that. Yet it was recommended as a great purchase for 'those who like eating out'.

A vigil outside the nearby St Mary's Hospital on Harrow Road was supported by the local vicar and several WEAG members. The hospital was to be turned into canalside luxury housing. This seemed to sum up everything that was wrong in 'Thatcher's Britain', as we liked to call it.

No one ever considered that house prices might drop – apart from my dad. Despite being retired, he still had the innate pessimism of the farmer who knows that the weather or the market could change at every turn. While I had never been in favour of parents buying houses for 21 year olds new to London, I was starting to feel increasingly desperate. Had my parents offered me a few thousand pounds to put down as a deposit, the proposal would have been considered and very probably grabbed.

However, when I visited my parents, not even the mention of the asbestos in my walls invoked offers of unconditional loans. My dad would just pour us each a glass of his rather palatable home brew (it worked out at four pence a pint). 'I've sawn asbestos pieces from my barns in half,' he'd say, as if this proved that its potential danger was a myth invented by pinko *Guardian* hacks.

He pointed out, reasonably enough, that all his money was needed for investments during his retirement. What if he lived to be 100? He was still amazed by house prices in London. 'There's no market in the world that can't go down as well as up,' he'd mutter darkly. My father was the only person I'd ever heard utter this heresy. Did he know something that Chancellor Nigel Lawson and the rest of the country didn't? Surely not. Little did I know that my dad was soon to be proved an economic genius.

In the summer of 1988, there was a huge rush to buy houses before multiple mortgage interest tax relief, known as MIRAS, was abolished in August. 'Get on the ladder before it's too late,' pleaded friends and workmates at pubs and dinner parties with all the warped obsessiveness of weirdo cult members, before recommending moving to somewhere like Clapton, which, in terms of accessibility by public transport, might as well have been western Papua New Guinea. There was a genuine whiff of housing hysteria in the air.

Whilst subbing at *Midweek*, people would tell me to move to Tottenham or buy with a friend, or even two, just as they were doing. It was all anyone could talk about. Regardless of the fact that friends fall out or have children and that shared property commitments are notoriously difficult to get out of. Never mind the Holy Cross. Or even King's Cross. Even I could see that moving to somewhere you hated with friends you might fall out with was not a sensible option. The ladder was everything in 1988, the sort of mythical structure that you'd imagine Harrison Ford searching for in lost South American citadels.

Ronald and I would sit in the Carlton plotting great escapes from short-life to permanent housing in London. Towards the end of 1988, Ronald got on his British bike (or at least the bits of it that were not in my flat) and did a Steve McQueen. Only this time he got through the barbed-wire defences, didn't answer 'thank you' in English and became a caretaker in a sheltered housing project in Hammersmith.

RENT BOY

My freelance career was prospering with regular commissions and subbing shifts. 'Pete May's condemned asbestos-ridden council gaff in the shadow of the Harrow Road flyover' made a number of appearances in the Editor's Chair section of *Midweek*, as bemused commuters heard ever more bizarre details of my picketing of City Hall in defence of some arrested councillors.

My annual profit from journalism was set to be around £10,000 from a £15,000 turnover, which was reasonable at the time. But with mortgage companies only offering three times your self-employed profit, this still left me tantalisingly short of getting a sufficient mortgage to buy a property. My savings were mounting, but not as fast as house prices were increasing. Nor would the banks and building societies even take into consideration the fact that I was now delivering leaflets for the local Labour Party free of charge in the hope of a more caring and fairer society.

My housing nemesis was partly my own fault too. If it was a choice between becoming an accountant to get a mortgage or trying to write, then it was the battered typewriter every time. Eleven years after the first Clash album, and now 28, this ageing punk was still determined not to grow up, calm down or find himself working for the clampdown.

It would all have been much easier with a partner, of course. It was impossible to buy without double incomes. The Conservative government had restored Victorian values all right and now it was marriage or short-life penury.

Unfortunately, by the late 1980s I had perfected the art of celibate affairs, spending numerous evenings in the company of women who only wanted to be friends. There was a brief liaison with someone from the Labour Party, but again, fine person that she undoubtedly was, our few evenings together were spent staring lovingly at her sumptuous flat. We'd sit in front of her designer fire discussing aromatherapy and shiatsu, as you did back then. It wasn't long before she went back to her old boyfriend.

Samantha Norman, daughter of the film critic Barry Norman, was working at *Midweek* at the time. Sam, a lovely person, arranged a hot lunchtime date with one of her friends, Anne, and we seemed to get on well. That summer, Anne invited me to the Edinburgh Festival and booked us into a shared room together. Everyone in the office thought that this confirmed a right result. Only when in our Edinburgh room I tentatively wondered if our shared room might constitute a come-on, she was enraged. She spent the next evening discussing the terrible sexism of my *Midweek* workmates with the prisoner-turned-playwright Jimmy Boyle, all in front of my chastened and still celibate self. It remains one of the worst nights of my life.

No wonder so many women dumped me; it must have been all those amorous glances at their front rooms. Or maybe it was just the asbestos particles over my jacket and the toxic odour of cockroach spray. I had purchased a TV from Rumbelows that worked so at least I was able to admire Sophie Aldred as Ace in *Doctor Who* without her appearing bright orange and five foot wide.

But at least work was exciting. My first-ever piece appeared in *The Guardian*. It was an interview with Gary Glitter, who seemed to my generation to be a cuddly old uncle figure. Years later, I'd discover that my judgement of celebrity heroes matched my property market abilities.

A greasy spoon off Ladbroke Grove hosted another of my *Midweek* interviews, this time with a favourite of mine, Joe Strummer. As Joe munched a melted cheese tuna sandwich and huskily explained why he was appearing in the Rock Against the Rich tour, I just wanted to grab him by the lapels of his leather jacket and exclaim: 'Joe, I've made it! Ten years after punk I'm living in a tower block under siege from Lady Porter! I'm on the front line!' Mind you, Joe was living in a family house in the posh end of Holland Park by then, so it was probably best that I didn't.

There was another strange encounter with a fellow tower-block occupant, Jeffrey Archer, the novelist and former chairman of the Conservative Party. His luxury flat was perched at the top of a private tower block on the banks of the Thames at Vauxhall. He even had a concierge instead of a graffiti-strewn lobby and piss-stained lift. As I arrived in my unironed shirt, the pristine Jeff proudly showed me the sweep of the Thames and his view across to the Houses of Parliament.

RENT BOY

On his glass coffee table stood numerous tomes such as *The French Impressionists*, *Cornish Painters*, *The Joy of Cricket*, *Watership Down* and *Hannibal's Footsteps*. Everything had its place: an immaculate polished grandfather clock, 14 works of art on the walls, gold-plated editions of all his works, his secretary typing quietly at her desk in the corner and Jeff's own desk with a high-tech lamp, a single flower in a vase and a gold pot in which all his pens were neatly placed. In short, it wasn't too dissimilar to my own gaff.

Archer was positively ebullient, having recently won a libel case over the ridiculous allegation that he slept with prostitute Monica Coughlan. 'How long have you been in the game then?' he boomed. At least I think he said 'in the game'. Alert to the art of flattering journalists, he asked me about my career and muttered things like 'Well done, sir!' and 'Good man!' Had he known of my ongoing battle with Lady Porter, he might not have been so impressed. Still, I thought, if he became prime minister one day, I might be able to use my new-found influence to save our estate.

I seemed to be leading a surreal double life, departing from my downwardly mobile council flat to interview soon-to-be mega celebrities. In December 1988, I met a young actress called Elizabeth Hurley who had just appeared in the BBC drama *Christabel*. Ronald's girlfriend 'Hotters' (as Liz called her) had attended the London Drama College with her and arranged the introduction. Liz had previously lived in the posh bit of Westbourne Park close to our toxic tower blocks. Even then she had played the part of the film star, parading down Westbourne Park Road with her poodle while still collecting her housing benefit.

At the time, she had moved into the Earls Court flat of some actor bloke called Hugh Grant. During the interview, her waste disposal unit was being repaired. It was an expensive-looking device that noisily crunched up all matter. The waste disposal unit at Hermes Point was less sophisticated consisting, as it did, of a chute and a festering pig bin. Liz made me a cup of tea and poured in some curdled milk from her fridge. 'Eeeergh, it looks like something from *Alien*!' she exclaimed.

Later in the interview, which was accompanied by the theme

from *The Singing Detective* on Liz's record player, Hugh Grant stumbled in. In his foppish manner, he announced that he'd just been for a burger. 'What an extraordinary thing to do,' mused Hurley. Even when she mentioned the 'ropey types' she'd encountered during her brief spell at a comprehensive school (common people like me!), I wasn't deterred. Clad in a baggy jumper and with her wonderful thick eyebrows (not the plucked version she has today), Liz was implausibly attractive.

At one point, she mentioned she'd like to marry a writer. If only I'd spoken out then and mentioned that I was currently available, Elizabeth's life might have been very different. Liz would have been installed in my short-life council flat, attending housing committee meetings and joining the residents' struggle to defend our homes. Hugh Grant would have been consigned to the refuse disposal chute of history and in those Hurley days, Liz and I would have enjoyed many a romantic evening supping real ale in the Carlton with the Group. But the words wouldn't come out, so it never happened. Elizabeth must still regret it.

As ever, my accommodation situation was tenuous and throughout the year there were rumours of impending eviction. The property market was still going into the stratosphere after the rush to buy before MIRAS was abolished.

In a move quite typical of the time, a property company planned to build so-called 'mingle units'. The mingle units were two-bedroom and two-bathroom houses, designed to attract people on joint incomes who couldn't afford to buy on their own. This had delightful connotations of Fry and Laurie types in smoking jackets and the odd *ménage à trois* in the style of the hugely popular Nescafé Gold Blend adverts. Only the property industry had already re-named bedsits as studio flats and back-to-backs as starter homes. Could a mingle unit be nothing more than what used to be termed 'houses of multiple occupation' or, even worse, 'flat-sharing'? I'd done my time in mingle units and I never wanted to return. Although, by 2000, we'd surely all be living in luxurious mingle cupboards.

On the positive side, we had seen off all attempts to remove us from the flats and ingeniously Walterton and Elgin Community Homes (WECH) had applied to take over the estates. Basically, it had inverted the government's legislation designed to promote privatisation of council homes by forming its own social housing company. There was the buzz of fighting a common enemy and a real sense of solidarity on the estates. As usual, a coach trip to hand in the bid ensured a big media presence. WECH had taken expert legal advice and in effect we could become the first tenants to own our own estate, an option that did not please City Hall.

Around this time, the tenants started to smell a WRAT. There were rumours of dirty tricks when a group called Westminster Residents Against Takeover emerged. The only three members of WRAT ready to be identified were two former tenants who had bought their council flats and one man who no longer lived on the estate but had been a member of Harrow Road ward Conservative Party. At a press conference, the three WRAT members stood before a picture of WECH leader Jonathan Rosenberg being arrested at a Westminster Council meeting when the Special Patrol Group were called in to clear the public gallery. Above the picture was the slogan 'Do you want this man as your landlord?'

They produced a seven-page dossier on Rosenberg's 'hard-left background' with cuttings dating back to 1985 which, in pre-Internet days, seemed to indicate some pretty sophisticated press monitoring techniques for 'ordinary working people'. After a little research, it soon became apparent that the address given by WRAT on its leaflets did not exist. Appropriately, WRAT then seemed to go underground, and one of its members was reduced to putting this message on his answer machine: 'This is a private number and nothing to do with WRAT.' No one knew who was really behind WRAT, but many had their suspicions.

Meanwhile, beyond the tower blocks it seemed that the asbestos had somehow leaked into the atmosphere and was corroding the fabric of society. Bad news was everywhere in the late 1980s: in 1987, the King's Cross station fire and the Zeebrugge ferry disaster; in 1988, a massive explosion on the Piper Alpha oil rig in the North Sea killing 167 people; in December that year, the Clapham Common train crash resulted in 36 deaths and there was the Lockerbie disaster with a death toll of 270. In January 1989, a British Midland jet crashed onto an embankment of the M1 killing over 50 people.

The only good news was that my accommodation situation appeared stable, just as higher inflation (6.4 per cent) was being fuelled by increased mortgage payments. The government pumped up interest rates from 8 to 12 per cent. The days of cheap low-interest mortgages were over and WECH was my last hope of finding affordable housing.

Early in 1989, my old mates from the Housing Corporation approved WECH as a designated landlord. They probably reasoned that if WECH could complete the byzantine HAR 10/2 form (with statistical appendix), then it could have as many estates as it wanted.

The other potential developers, not so keen on the idea of bus-loads of lefties occupying their offices, had quietly withdrawn. It would surely be impossible for the council to evict members of a group that was attempting to buy their own estate. It seemed that we had won.

But we underestimated Lady Porter and Westminster Council. It was a juggernaut that was coming our way and would not be diverted. There it was on the doormat. It had finally arrived on 3 March 1989. My notice to quit in 28 days. Eviction was embracing me once again.

MORTGAGE PROSPECTS: The applicant should be aware that house prices in London are going up by 26 per cent per annum. He has been sacked from his low-paid job, which is looked upon unfavourably by most lenders. The applicant is now on the Enterprise Allowance Scheme and receiving some earnings from freelance journalism in the middle of a property boom in the most expensive borough in the country. Furthermore, he is soon to be of no fixed abode. The applicant has as much chance of joining the property-owning democracy as Lady Porter has of being signed up by the Workers' Revolutionary Party.

AVERAGE HOUSE PRICE IN GREATER LONDON: £96,414

9. The Most Dangerous Tower Block in Britain

17th Floor, Hermes Point, Westbourne Park, London W9
May 1989 to November 1990

'DANGER, THESE COUNCIL FLATS CAN KILL: Asbestos dust peril revealed' read the front page of the *Daily Mirror* on 7 July 1990. On pages four and five it continued: 'THE MOST DANGEROUS FLATS IN BRITAIN: The tower block where even squatters won't live.' There was a picture of a council 'technician' in a white spacesuit and gas mask testing the heating vent of one of the Hermes Point flats. The council's men had to dress in lunar exploration gear for their visits, but homeless families, tenants and short-lifers were expected to live there. Another shot of Hermes Point had the caption: 'Tower of Fear'.

It was a great tabloid scoop. The *Mirror* highlighted the fact that Tory Westminster Council had just moved scores of homeless families into the blocks. It reported that when they moved in, most of them were completely unaware of the dangers of the brown asbestos and many had already drilled holes in the walls. Labour councillors claimed the council's decision was a way of scuppering WECH's bid to take over the estates by removing the short-life licensees and was also a strategy to shift likely Labour voters from marginal wards to a safe Labour ward.

There were photos of exposed asbestos in a burnt-out flat at 100 Hermes Point and WECH's Jonathan Rosenberg described pigeons as having made nests out of the asbestos. A homeless family was about to be moved next door to two burnt-out flats at numbers 92 and 93. With all those blackened flats, the block really did look like a scene from Beirut. No doubt Terry Waite, at the time kidnapped in Lebanon, would eventually be found inside. The *Mirror* also discovered council documents from 1983 and 1985 warning of the dangers of asbestos within the blocks. The only two other blocks of the same design were in Tower Hamlets where tenants had already been moved out.

The council denied there was any problem, of course. Westminster's director of the housing department told the *Mirror*: 'If there was a real risk to families we would not have put them there. I took the view that the flats were of good use and better than bed and breakfast accommodation.' Westminster's deputy director of environmental health told the paper: 'There is no suggestion that air levels are in any way dangerous. The council has a very clear asbestos policy. If the asbestos is sealed and not damaged then the risks are minimised.' Which all sounded as reassuring as Nigel Lawson's protestations that he was in complete support of Margaret Thatcher.

Labour councillor Gavin Millar, a polished barrister and fine advocate during the struggle, summed it up with the comment: 'It is a typical Westminster story. Pounds, shillings and pence seem to be the most important thing to them.'

Right. So maybe my decision to stay on in Hermes Point hadn't been that sound. The fact that I was officially living in one of the most dangerous tower blocks in Britain even made the *UK Press Gazette*. Steve Platt, the former editor of *Midweek* and soon-to-be supremo at the *New Statesman*, wrote: 'Where the squatter fears to tread, the journalist makes his bed.' It seemed I had gained more journalistic credibility than even the most hardened of war correspondents simply through having a dodgy council gaff on the Harrow Road.

My eviction from my second-floor flat in Hermes Point in May 1989 had been traumatic. Just about the only thing that has ever prevented me sleeping properly is property concerns. Nothing worries you quite like the simple loss of the roof over your head. All I'd ever wanted was a secure rented place to live in London. And now, just like in *When Harry Met Sally*, I was going to be 'out there again', in the private rental market.

Having been busy boarding up empty council houses and selling them off to yuppies – at the same time trying to ship the homeless out to the badlands of Essex and other distant counties – the council was now very enthusiastic about housing homeless families in our asbestos-ridden tower blocks, simultaneously creating 150 homeless short-lifers, who were all members of WECH. It was a cynical manipulation of the homeless – and to be defined as homeless by the council you needed kids, who would be at greater risk from being exposed to asbestos at such a young age. Even on a practical level, it seemed the council couldn't be listening to the advice of its own housing officers. Anyone with any experience of housing management would have known that clearing 75 flats in 28 days just wasn't possible.

The WECH members in the other short-life housing associations took the only possible action – they created another acronym. SHOUT stood for Short-Lifers Under Threat. Its members refused to move anywhere and challenged the eviction notice through the courts. Our first victory was when we discovered that the eviction notices were incorrectly worded, which gave us another month at least while they were served again.

The Group now had six flats and the other members wanted to cooperate as much as possible with the council. Perhaps I should have squatted in my flat in the manner of the SHOUT members, but I was under a considerable moral obligation to the Group not to jeopardise their relationship with Westminster. They had offered me cheap housing when I was desperate.

Eventually, the council did offer the Group replacement short-life flats on the Walterton estate. One or two of them were decent places, but the basement flat that I was offered was the sort of gaff that even Withnail and I would have rejected.

A former junkies' squat, it had needles over the floor, smashed-out windows, no bathroom, no hot water and filth and rubble everywhere. Not having a bathroom seemed too much like a real return to Victorian values. I would exchange like for like, but not this.

The rest of the Group said I was mad, but in truth my confidence had gone. I didn't believe I'd be able to supervise or afford building a bathroom or fitting new windows, doors and wiring or the myriad other jobs that were needed to make the flat habitable.

It also felt wrong to be quitting the fight. What Thatcherism as a whole, and Westminster Council in particular, was doing was wrong. Like the miners in 1985, I wanted to do the right thing, even if it meant eventual defeat. Now was the moment to fight Lady Porter for my right to graft at the typeface.

A solution to the dilemma came when another short-life housing association that had numerous flats in the tower blocks offered me a place. It wasn't perfect, as I'd be sharing again. It was a place in a two-bedroom flat on the seventeenth floor, which the housing association had turned into a three-bedroom flat by fitting a flimsy partition across the living room. However, the rent was still only around £40 a month and my new flatmates, Sally and Chris, seemed good people. Sally was a nurse who'd been active in WECH and SHOUT, while Chris was a graduate turned gardener at a park in Ealing.

Even so, it was a dark and mournful May morning when the men came to put the Sitex door on the first flat that I'd ever possessed on my own. Even the cockroaches looked tearful. Scraps of typewritten articles and dubious dust littered the floor of my toxic home. To compound the agony, just as I was clearing the final remnants, a feral-looking character barged through the open Sitex door and announced 'You moving out? Go on, mate, give us the keys!'

I explained in as simple a manner as I could manage that the keys had to be returned to the council by my housing association. By this time, I was probably looking quite dangerous because the Sitex scavenger eventually left, without the need for propulsion from my Dr. Martens. And so I handed the keys back to DHO7, the sort of futuristic-sounding destination which Douglas Adams would surely have used as a transmat port.

My room on the 17th floor of Hermes Point was still large

compared to private-sector boxes, even if it was sometimes disconcerting to think that my bed by the exterior wall was just a few inches away from a 17-storey drop. At times, the vivid pink sunsets over the city were stunning and it felt like being in an exclusive penthouse – just as long as you didn't think about the lifts outside or the burnt-out places a couple of floors above us. Sally and Chris proved to be as adept at drinking in the Carlton as the Group. There were neighbourhood parties and SHOUT meetings as an impasse was reached with the council.

In the outside world, the economy was slumping. Inflation reached 8 per cent in May 1989 and interest rates were rising too. All those people who rushed to buy houses in Tottenham were starting to squeal over their increased mortgage payments. The property market was levelling out, as the building societies would put it.

In reality, prices in London were starting to fall. My dad had been right all along. What I thought had been unfounded property market pessimism over pints of home brew had turned out to be financial wisdom. The property boom had been a chimera. The illusion of wealth and making money simply from sitting on a property for a few months rather than producing any goods or services had gone.

A sensible person would have carried on saving for a deposit on a flat. However, the emotional trauma of moving had left me exhausted and I decided to visit my sister Pam in Australia, something I had planned to do for many years. She'd left England when she was 19 and had long ago bought her own flat in Perth. My other sister Kaz, who was ten years younger than me, had moved in with her boyfriend in Dagenham and was now an official council tenant. Even in my own family, I was at the bottom of the property ladder.

That June, I'd written a feature for *Midweek* on the American evangelist Billy Graham speaking at West Ham's Upton Park ground, where he had at least prayed for the relegated Hammers. He used a quote from Ernest Hemingway about 'when everything you've ever wanted wasn't enough'. Something was missing from my life, too. Not God, but a permanent, affordable flat.

RENT BOY

During the summer of 1989, a heatwave hit the capital and every few days I'd find myself walking to my subbing shifts at *Midweek* as the Tube drivers called one-day strikes. West Ham had just been relegated. My 30th birthday was approaching and I wanted to escape. What price property over experience?

Sally and Chris were happy to hold my room over the summer and were left pre-paid cheques for the still very cheap rent. So from July to October this rent boy was on the highway in Oz. As I travelled to Perth, Derby, Darwin, Katherine, Ayers Rock and Sydney it was glorious to leave behind the worries of short-life living. It was possible to live out of a backpack for six months without property or possessions.

There was a sense of space in Australia and what really struck me – and yes, we're getting the impression of a man obsessed here – was the size of the houses. Even the equivalent of a local authority flat had three bedrooms and a huge garden. And when you met other travellers from England, it was surprising how many were running away from the country's property market. Even while I travelled, disasters continued to fill the front pages: the sinking of the *Marchioness* and, of course, the Ashes.

My sister was temporarily living on Koolan Island off the western coast near Derby. Her boyfriend worked for a mining company. From his free company house with air conditioning, there were amazing views of ancient red cliffs, glistening mud and a beach with what seemed like the biggest tidal range in the world. At night, bush fires snaked and shimmered across the mainland. The Southern Cross and countless other stars were clear in the sky, 12,000 miles away from the light pollution of London.

But money was finite and having blown several thousand pounds and any hope of scaling the property ladder for several more years, this long-term renter returned to autumnal England. Just in time to see interest rates reach an astonishing 15 per cent, the Berlin Wall fall, the end of the Cold War and the arrival of BSE. But even in these fluctuating times, Lady Porter was somehow still in power. Who would rid us of this turbulent piece?

Sally had moved in with her new Italian boyfriend so Chris and

THE MOST DANGEROUS TOWER BLOCK IN BRITAIN

I were left alone in the flat. We both agreed that the flats were too small to cram in an extra person and so whenever our housing association sent round a prospective flatmate we simply emphasised the dangers of the asbestos and the piles of washing up in our sink.

Chris was the sort of character who would eventually find his way into a Nick Hornby book: as well as working as a park-keeper in Ealing, he helped run a second-hand record shop and stall in Portobello Market. He knew about new outfits such as The Stone Roses and the Manic Street Preachers, and acid house (which was more than I did), and could tell you the sale or exchange price of any piece of vinyl. He would rise very early to go to his park-keeper's job and stay up very late drinking in the Portobello Gold or Lonsdale pubs, or going to gigs. Hence his amiable air of bewilderment whenever we stumbled across each other in the living room.

His job as Percy the Park-keeper suited him. It also made a fine feature for *Midweek* when I spent the day with his park gang. Chris and his eccentric workmates would spend much of their day dodging a mad park regular and acid casualty who called himself the Sulphur Vulcan of Avalon. Chris was known as ALF (which stood for Alien Life Form) by the rest of his colleagues. Mind you, they had equally unlikely monikers such as Storky (a Goth gardener with bright red hair who had a boa constrictor as a pet), Peregrine Dorrell the Food Fiend (a connoisseur of vindaloos), Skippy (an inveterate skip-diver), the Carrot Man (a vegetarian), Technopath (into software), the Dog Slayer (he hated dogs) and Captain Bob, who wasn't actually a gardener but a rough sleeper who seemed to have joined their gang.

During my day with them we spent the early hours on death row (so named because it was always ten degrees colder than any other part of the park), several hours trying to uproot a shrub and the rest of the day sheltering from the rain in caffs staffed by Dot Cotton lookalikes, while trying to escape the attention of the Führer (their foreman). Early starts aside, it wasn't the most taxing of jobs; it could be performed with a hangover and allowed Chris to dream of

'70s band Television's green-vinyl 12-inch singles while wielding his axe at shrubs.

We were still living under the threat of eviction, but at least I was only nearly homeless. That Christmas, I wrote a piece for *The Guardian* about doing a charity sleep-out in aid of the charity Homes for Homeless People. Around 30 volunteers kipped on market tables around the back of St Martin-in-the-Fields Church, just off Trafalgar Square.

A passer-by suddenly stopped to take in the scene as I posed for the *Guardian* photographer with my sleeping bag round my shoulders, huddling against the freezing grey stones of the church as the rain spattered the paving slabs. The spectator was clearly aghast at the image. 'That's London life, mate,' he muttered to the photographer, shaking his head. Yes, I looked more convincing as a homeless person than the homeless themselves.

We ate sandwiches donated at the end of the day by Cranks restaurant and huddled in our sleeping bags. Only the cold seemed to pierce every layer and there was no chance of sleeping. A burger-chomping 19 year old from Manchester accused us of being middle class (which was quite true) and ridiculed the idea that after one night we would know what it's like to be homeless. 'I've been begging and that's as low as you can get, apart from prostitution,' he told us. He then pulled out a copy of *City Limits* and went to look for a good club.

A young Ulster-born skinhead thanked us for what we were doing and said that in south London all the council housing went to 'IRA supporters and Pakis'. He played in a reggae band but said the black members in it were all right because they were his mates.

Any attempt to sleep was interrupted by the noise of the demonstrators outside the nearby South African embassy wanting to free Nelson Mandela and end apartheid. There was also a drunken Glaswegian called Soldier with a wooden walking stick who abused us all night shouting, 'fookin students' and worse. He sprayed beer over us, muttered that he was in the army and sang broken snatches of 'Let's Dance' while graphically describing the sexual activities he had planned for the women among us. That is until he slashed his stick at a Liverpudlian woman who leapt out of her bag and threatened to cuff him. Soldier meekly retreated.

But it was the small things that I found exasperating, such as finding the loos in Charing Cross station shut and the 'superloo' jammed. No wonder those sleeping on the streets had to urinate wherever they could. Youths wandered around with blankets over their shoulders looking like Buddhist monks. At 6 a.m., we got our sponsorship forms signed and retreated home. Warm gusts of air gushed from the ventilator on the wall in Hermes Point as I collapsed onto my bed. Whatever was wrong with Hermes Point, it was home; a luxury thousands of people in the country didn't have.

By the time 1990 arrived, Chancellor Nigel Lawson had already resigned and Margaret Thatcher seemed to be steering the economy about as well as her son Mark was navigating his way through the Sahara desert. January saw a record trade deficit of £20 billion and recession looming.

However, Pete May was making his first venture into information technology and purchased an Amstrad hard-drive computer to replace his electric typewriter. Grey screen, mind you, not green. It was a bizarre new modem world. Was Dot Matrix a cousin of Dot Cotton? Was an auto exec bat file something that Michael Keaton kept down his utility belt in *Batman*? Were logic bombs something Mr Spock threw at Klingons? What were a deep-scan burst nibbler, vectorisation, bitmapping and non-volatile RAM and why did they all sound like they had been thought up by the geekiest of science fiction fans who had spent their childhoods getting harassed by psychopathic games masters who looked like Brian Glover in *Kes*? Probably because they were. All I really needed was Tom Baker's sonic screwdriver to properly install my Amstrad and I'd be fine.

Life drifted on through pub visits and SHOUT meetings and poll tax riots and West Ham losing 6–0 to Oldham on Valentine's Day. Vicky at *Ms London* did her best to fix me up. She was eventually to become editor of *Time Out* and then a crucial figure on *Now!* magazine, and was part of what editor-in-chief Bill Williamson referred to as 'the sisterhood' on *Ms London*. His editorials would frequently refer to 'Miss Vicky stuffing fivers down her bodice' as she attempted to find Pete May hot dates. Sadly, she never had much success.

Hardly a freelance sub was allowed to escape the office without being quizzed about their thoughts on campaigning journalist Pete May, but strangely none of them seemed to have any interest in getting into my asbestos-bleached underwear, particularly the ones from the likes of *Prima* and *19*.

Then the month of May brought ominous news. Much hope had been placed on Labour winning the council elections and letting WECH take over the estates. I'd even written a document called 'Westminster's Dirty Dozen' for the Labour Party which was launched with some razzmatazz by Bryan Gould. But it made no difference. Seduced by a ridiculously low poll-tax rate, the rich voters of Westminster voted the Conservatives back in.

In any case, it seemed that we were being beaten by the buildings themselves. WECH had done its own survey and the asbestos situation was much worse than we had thought. There was eight and a half miles of the stuff in the blocks and loose fibres were being detected in flat surveys. Chris and I followed WECH's advice to turn off the heater boosters, fill up the gaps around the beams and cover the wall joins with masking tape. At last, I was being forced to learn how to do DIY. I should have known – in *Doctor Who* the monster always comes up to get you through the ventilation shaft.

Asbestos is nasty stuff. The microscopic fibres can get into your lungs and cause lung cancers, such as mesothelioma, but often the symptoms don't emerge until 30-odd years later. Clearly we were at less risk than if we had smoked, or worked with asbestos. In 1997, a report by Professor Julian Peto commissioned by WECH and Westminster Council concluded that there was a 1 in 20 chance that a single extra cancer would occur among the 3,000 ex-residents of the Points. Even so, the search for affordable housing in London may end up killing one or more of the former tower blocks' residents. The greater the time in the buildings, the more the risk. Who knows what future research might unearth? The short-lifers had been led to believe that the tower blocks were relatively safe. Yet now we're all living with a life sentence of fear.

Nelson Mandela had been freed after nearly 27 years of incarceration and I was beginning to feel I might be stuck in Hermes Point for a similar length of time. Then 'THE MOST DANGEROUS FLATS IN BRITAIN' story broke in the *Mirror*. A couple of months later, the phone line in the flat went dead and the BT engineers refused to enter the building to repair it. I had become the only phoneless freelance journalist in Britain. By August, there were air monitors in our hallway. Even the hardiest of us asbestos-dwellers began to accept that it was time to leave.

Just as my own housing hopes seemed to be imploding, the property market as a whole was doing a very good impression of one of those tower blocks being demolished with a ceremonial push of the button. Interest rates were still catastrophically high for borrowers and inflation was running at nearly 9 per cent.

For 11 years, the Tory government had given us the illusion of prosperity. 'But Mrs Thatcher's created wealth, my house has gone up £20,000!' someone once told me. Yes, but these people never seemed to realise that if your house went up then it would cost you even more to buy somewhere else. No goods or services had been created. Many estate agents had got rich and their huge commissions had helped to fuel the endless price hikes, but overall the housing-led consumer boom had been created with money we didn't have.

Now the only people worse off than me were those who had rushed to buy before the abolition of multiple mortgage interest tax relief in 1988. Britain was being hit by a wave of negative equity. In the first six months of the year, there had been 14,390 repossessions. If your house was repossessed and sold you could not only lose your deposit but also be sued by the building societies and banks for the fall in value. The one thing the worshippers of the free market had forgotten to tell us was that in any market, property prices could go down as well as up. For the first time since the Second World War, property prices were in decline.

It all seemed evidence of a country gone mad. In Europe and the USA there was nothing like the same obsession with home ownership and there was no disgrace attached to the idea of renting an apartment for most of your life. And so much depended on being a couple. It seemed that the property market of the previous decade had done more for the institution of marriage than the Pope. The Church of England should have been campaigning for ever higher interest rates just to ensure that no one ever dared lead a single life again.

In London, there were an estimated 75,000 people homeless (with 10,000 on the streets) and nationally Shelter estimated 1 million people were without a roof over their heads. The virtual abolition of council housing, the care in the community patients who found that the community didn't care and ended up sleeping rough, the changes in regulations that made it even more difficult for young people to claim social security – it was a hopeless cocktail of housing despair.

Reluctantly, I began the search for accommodation yet again. With great optimism, I placed an advert in *Midweek*. Surely some benevolent landlord would have read my pieces, decide I was the next George Orwell and offer a ridiculously cheap home to a pioneering young journalist? Strangely, no one did. An advert in *Loot* resulted in a trip to a dodgy private flat in Kilburn that seemed to have its bedroom, bathroom and living room in entirely random areas of the landlord's house. Unused to the ruthlessness of the private lettings market, I hesitated over a £100-a-week basement flat in Islington and it was gone.

In desperation, I even went to see a building society about getting a mortgage. As usual they refused to have any sympathy for the self-employed. And, having previously been so keen to lend buyers three and a half times their income, they were now reducing their offers to two and a half times their income in the face of negative equity, repossessions and a 10 per cent inflation rate. Then Norman Lamont, the new Chancellor with a curious badger haircut, attempted to take Britain into the ERM (although why he wanted to join a cult American band I'll never know) and then withdrew quicker than any of the many sleazy Tory MPs practising *coitus interruptus* with their research assistants.

THE MOST DANGEROUS TOWER BLOCK IN BRITAIN

I was about as welcome to the building societies as Inspector Chisholm in the Winchester Club in *Minder*. The society's grand offer was a total mortgage of £24,000 when I needed at least £60,000 or £70,000 to buy a flat. Even if they had considered my turnover rather than my profit, it would still have been far too little.

Chris and I were in a cycle of untogether mediocrity, although sometimes Chris's amiable lack of togetherness after the previous night's overindulgence and a day at the park suggested that he'd probably think Asbestos Dust was a hot new indie band. He was planning on making his own accommodation arrangements with one of the mad gardeners from Ealing. Even the Sulphur Vulcan of Avalon would be preferable to this.

Finally, after three fruitless months, my housing association came up with a flat on a Peabody estate in SW1. It was solid, only required a little painting and as far as I could see it had no cancer-inducing substances within its walls. This was to be my escape to Victoria.

On 22 November 1990, Margaret Thatcher resigned, after her own party rebelled against her. That lunchtime, I was subbing at *ROOF*. My struggle to find somewhere decent to live was, unlike Margaret Thatcher, destined to go on and on. Instead of celebrating on the streets, I was packing boxes.

In that day's *Standard*, one of the most prominent adverts in the flats and maisonettes for sale section read: 'Repossession property available, St John's Wood, luxury flats and houses, serious principals only'. There was Mrs Thatcher's fall in microcosm; the British had discovered that there was no such thing as ever-increasing property prices. The market could not be bucked.

On 29 November, I moved out of Hermes Point, after four years and three months of tower-block living. Slowly, the blocks were emptying as the asbestos rain carried on pissin' down. Last one out, press the detonation button.

There's a famous scene in *Whatever Happened to the Likely Lads?* where Bob and Terry return to the haunts of their youth only to find the bulldozers busy demolishing their past. It felt like that when in

2004 I returned to the site of Hermes Point with Ronald. As we viewed the new panorama, I mused, 'You see this, once it was all tower blocks.'

Hermes and Chantry Points had been demolished in 1994. In their place stood a road called Hermes Close and new four-storey low-rise flats. The residents had their own doctor's surgery and there was a plush new office for WECH. Another close was called Victory Court. For WECH had won. All those people who had said there was no chance of victory against Lady Porter and Westminster Council were wrong. The arrests, the legal battles, the evictions – ultimately it had all been worthwhile and the old council tenants were in decent, affordable housing. Fifty-five new homes have been built on the site of the old tower blocks.

In 1994, Lady Porter was surcharged £27 million after the district auditor Don Magill accused her of 'wilful misconduct' and 'disgraceful gerrymandering' in the 1990 'homes for votes' scandal. Westminster Council was accused of selling off council homes in eight marginal wards in order to prevent Labour gaining power in the 1990 elections.

In 1996, the independent Barratt Report concluded that the council had 'showed a lack of proper care' in exposing the residents to asbestos. Barratt also concluded that 'the major informal policy which dominated all decision making' about both Hermes and Chantry Point was the defeat of the takeover bid by WECH and that 'No adequate thought was given nor adequate advice taken in relation to current asbestos risk.'

The report stated that moving homeless families into the blocks was a strategy to 'destroy the financial viability of WECH's bid'. The council believed that the homeless families would place WECH in an awkward position if they won. It would have had to reduce its repair programme because of the cost of rehousing all the homeless families, or evict them, attracting bad publicity. Barratt also reported that the homeless families were given 'no information or advice about the asbestos materials' and when information was made available 'the assurance of safety was extravagant'.

THE MOST DANGEROUS TOWER BLOCK IN BRITAIN

Barratt concluded that 'those acting on behalf of a public body repeatedly took risks for a variety of reasons with the health of people who ought to have been entitled to assume that such risks were not being taken'.

The narrow politics of Westminster came before the health of homeless people. It is hard to think of any elected council acting in a more disgusting and contemptuous fashion. Today, the WECH homes on the Walterton and Elgin estates are proof that sometimes the little people can win.

MORTGAGE PROSPECTS: Even without a phone, the applicant's freelance earnings are increasing. However, he must be aware that the days of building societies and banks lending gullible fools three and a half times their income are over. Spending several thousand pounds on travelling to Australia was extremely ill-advised with regard to the current temperature of the housing market. Exposure to asbestos does not recommend him as a long-term risk either. As the applicant's profit figures are still consistently too low to buy anything other than a one-bedroom flat in Middlesbrough, we suggest he gets a permanent, pensionable job.

AVERAGE HOUSE PRICE IN GREATER LONDON: £92,558

10. Escape to Victoria

Abbey Orchard Estate, Victoria, London SW1
December 1990 to November 1991

'Homelessness was still a huge problem in 1990' read the caption in *The Guardian's* New Year review in early 1991. Above it was a huge picture of Pete May, dosser. Somehow the picture *The Guardian* had taken of me sleeping rough for charity in January 1990 had entered their picture files as a picture of a real homeless person. What was most worrying was that out of *The Guardian's* entire library of photos, the picture editor must have thought that the most authentic and dramatic picture illustrating the terrible blight and misery of the homeless in the UK was one of me. Was it just the effects of a long lunch at *Midweek* or prolonged exposure to asbestos that had given my face such a deathly pallor? Did I really look that desperate?

Maybe I did, for it was a huge relief to move into a new flat without (as far as I knew) any life-threatening substances concealed in its walls. It was as if an asbestos cloud had been lifted. Michael Palin had just reinvented himself as a good-humoured quintessentially English traveller in his TV series *Around the World in 80 Days* and I felt like I'd done the same, albeit in slightly harsher circumstances. Palin might have braved intransigent camels, locomotives and liners, but he'd surely never have had the resilience to stay in Hermes Point.

There were some withdrawal symptoms, though. Suddenly there

131

were no more SHOUT meetings, no leafleting sessions organised from the Labour rooms opposite the tower block and no more picketing of Lady Porter. A sense of community had been lost. But moving would certainly be better for my mental health. That December, a former member of the Group mentioned that during the past year I seemed like I'd been 'chewed up by life'. And if a member of the Group thought you were chewed up by life, then there was surely no hope left.

Abbey Orchard estate, just off Abbey Orchard Street, was built after the Great Fire of 1666 on the site of Westminster Abbey's medieval orchard. These days it wasn't as bucolic as it sounded, being set just off the constant flow of traffic and pedestrians along Victoria Street.

The housing association had found me a good solid flat on a Peabody estate, even if the letter 'L' above the archway on the communal staircase did make it seem a bit like *Prisoner Cell Block H*. The proper Peabody residents seemed to be mainly old people who kept mainly to their flats. Each block had an interior courtyard with trees and it was all very sedate and pleasant after Hermes Point.

The Victorian walls of the flats were reassuringly solid and, although there were only bare floorboards and peeling bad-taste wallpaper, with a little work it would be fine. Apparently the flats would be available for a year, while they awaited the installation of central heating, fitted bathrooms and kitchens, and entry phones. As most building projects were invariably late, there was hope that we short-lifers might be in residence much longer.

Peabody buildings were all across London, with the Peabody Trust managing nearly 12,000 properties on 72 estates. They were built with money from a trust set up by the American philanthropist George Peabody. In the 1860s, he donated £500,000 to 'ameliorate the condition of the poor and needy of this great metropolis and to promote their comfort and happiness'. Much of the trust's money was put into housing blocks for 'the artisan and labouring poor', which seemed pretty much like a perfect description of life as a freelance journalist. At the time, the housing was thought to be quite austere but, after years renting in London, these 'cheap, cleanly, well-drained and healthful dwellings for the poor' seemed positively palatial to an itinerant hack like myself.

Finally, Pete May had an SW1 address – which was impressive on paper at least. The flats were a short walk from Victoria station along Victoria Street, and also very close to Westminster Abbey, Downing Street and the Houses of Parliament, should Neil Kinnock ever need me as his 'yoof' consultant. Sir Robin Day could be seen buying his groceries in Europa on Victoria Street. This was Westminster Village and I was at its heart.

The pubs were packed at six o'clock and as my pal Paul worked for the Water Services Association across the road in Queen Anne's Gate there were plenty of opportunities for medicinal lunchtime and after-work drinks. By the late evening, the area was eerily quiet though. At least I could sleep, particularly as none of my new neighbours had decided to welcome me with a vase through the window.

I had initially moved in with a friend from the same housing association. When she moved out, for the first time in my life, I pulled a housing scam. Simply through carrying on paying her rent I could have the flat to myself. The housing association would not lose out financially and I would have space for an office from which to work. This was probably deeply iniquitous, but even the staunchest of idealists are eventually worn down by the perpetual struggle for some form of housing security.

Sod ethics: that was a county somewhere beyond Barking. Lady Porter's nemesis had succumbed to 'roofless' ambition. I was flat-shared out and working from home gave me special needs, I reasoned. There were people who had done much worse. At many a London dinner party, you'd hear of people who had given false addresses to join housing associations, or lied about their income. And at least I wasn't sub-letting the place to a Tory MP in need of a love nest. After those idealistic days of black Levi 501s, we all found ourselves clad in selfish jeans now.

There was plenty to do in the flat. Despite being as effective at DIY as Frank Spencer, I managed to buy some paint and stepladders. The bedroom was painted designer white, just like my style counsellor Vicky at *Ms London* had advocated. My attempts at varnished floors were even more successful. Forget sanding and all that nonsense. It was much easier to simply buy some dark varnish and daub it onto the floorboards that were exposed around the edge of my big blue rug. Admittedly, there was a large square patch of unvarnished floorboard beneath the rug, but no one would know and the builders would soon be gutting it anyway.

The Peabody blocks were just a few hundred yards away from the Abbey Orchard market where a variety of cheap plastic kitchen utensils, pots and pans and bargain *Doctor Who* videos at £4.99 each could be found, so soon my new home was almost complete. Further succumbing to the spirit of the '90s, I even bought a filter coffee machine from the market. At last I could be like the Group, drinking real coffee in my social housing. An air of optimism arrived with 1991. Surely my romantic life would improve now that my female guests no longer feared imminent attacks from asbestos-drenched cockroaches, visits from men in white spacesuits with Geiger counters or Lady Porter turning up with a vase.

In early January, Ronald and myself, still old gits around town, hit a social workers' party held by a friend of Ronald's. It was there that I met Joanne. She was a probation officer and seemed to like the fact that I was not a career criminal. On our first date, we had dinner at a posh restaurant in St James's Park, close to my flat.

Iraq had invaded Kuwait and the Western allies were striking back. On the night that Operation Desert Storm began, fearing the implications of war and Saddam Hussein's chemical weapons, we kissed in the rain on Westminster Bridge in view of Parliament, perhaps watched by a bemused John Major. He was, after all, a devoted family man who didn't go in for that sort of thing.

Joanne and I were good for each other, even if at times her life did seem to be like something from a Ken Loach film. She was a single mother with two children, both with different dads. In her spare time, she was a rock climber. And she had a proper house on Brixton Hill with three bedrooms, a garden, a cellar, a tree in the front garden, a hob, pine bookshelves and a Bodem cafetière.

The only problem was her ex-boyfriend came with it too. Eric was the father of her first child, seven-year-old Cerys. They had bought the house together and despite splitting up were still living together, in separate rooms. He was an amiable rocket scientist and *Doctor Who* fan, so we actually got on quite well. He could even do DIY. One day, I found him changing the plumbing in the bathroom, remarking that it was merely a case of 'following first principles'. If it had been me, the whole of Brixton would have been saturated.

Superficially, Eric didn't seem to mind the arrangement too much, although it did seem decidedly weird to be staying in Joanne's room while he was sleeping a couple of doors along the corridor. To complicate it some more, he had a new girlfriend who would also sleep over with her daughter. We were definitely all very grown up about relationships in Brixton's largest extended family.

Maybe it was just a symptom of the London property market: with negative equity, you were stuck with your ex-partners, whether you wanted to live with them or not. Joanne's second child was Daisy, a lovely two year old. Her father was a man called Phil, who had lived with Joanne, but had scarpered as soon as she became pregnant.

Joanne supplied me with some old wicker blinds for the curtainless windows in my new gaff. She introduced me to Bodems and pesto; and the fact that life with children is richer but bloody knackering. We'd walk through St James's Park with Daisy swinging between our arms as she cooed at the ducks. Each morning at 6 a.m. there would be a mini Operation Desert Storm on the landing as Daisy pounded across the bare floorboards shouting 'I want bekfist!' followed by 'Poohy!' and 'Wake up, Pizza!' (by which she meant me). Cerys would meanwhile announce that she wasn't going to school and Joanne would explain that she was a probation officer and was legally obliged to send her children there. It was chaotic, but in a strange way enjoyable, and made me aware that perhaps I had dad potential.

Back in Victoria, it was starting to feel a little unsafe. In February, the IRA had blasted Downing Street with mortars and then bombed nearby Victoria station. At the same time, my employment prospects were looking as hopeful as the chances of John Major turning out to be a secret sex god.

In March, unemployment topped two million and numerous magazines were folding or cutting staff. The likes of *Sounds* and *Record Mirror* were among the high-profile casualties and every publication was cutting its freelance budget. Along with Tim Southwell (later to be the co-founder of *Loaded*), I lost my two-days-a-week regular subbing at *Midweek*. We had been downsized.

Gleefully, I cut out a cartoon from *The Guardian* and stuck it on my new cork office noticeboard. It parodied the old Saatchi & Saatchi 'Labour Isn't Working' ad. This one read 'The Media Isn't Working' and pictured a huge line of 'meeja' types queuing outside the dole office.

Still, as some terrible song of the time reminded me, when the going gets tough, the tough get going and, slowly, after a couple of very lean months and much grovelling to increasingly juvenile-looking features editors, some new outlets and sources of commissions emerged.

One of my journalistic highlights from the time was meeting *Doctor Who*'s Nicholas Courtney, Sophie Aldred and many other *Who* stars at the launch of the Behind the Sofa exhibition at the Museum of the Moving Image. While the monitors flashed images of imploding cybermen and giant maggots in Welsh quarries, the thought occurred to me that the Tardis was just another form of short-life housing. No wonder the Doctor had left Gallifrey to become a wanderer in the Fifth Dimension; evicted by the Timelords, he had become a galactic rough sleeper.

Talking of rough sleeping, my Victoria flat was immensely convenient for my next charity sleep-out outside Westminster Cathedral. And at least this one was in July. Your designer dosser merely had to saunter a few hundred yards from his SW1 flat to join an assortment of luvvies on the streets.

Jeremy Irons was there, sleeping in a cardboard box in front of the cathedral. With his lank hair and gaunt features he looked rougher than most of the actual homeless. Alongside him were the likes of Emma Freud, Janet Suzman, Kenny Lynch, Peter Bottomley MP, Len Murray, Libby Purves and Clive Soley MP. It was a bit like a decade-early pilot for *I'm A Celebrity Get Me Out of Here!* Each of their boxes had a sticker for National Sleep-Out Week on it. There were crash barriers around the sleeping celebs to separate them from the real homeless and a policeman was on guard.

Billy Bragg was there too. 'I can't get arrested, I'm on *Top of the Pops* tomorrow!' he quipped. He protested against the social apartheid by going to join the real homeless people kipping by McDonald's, where a vent from the kitchens provided gusts of warm air. 'I'm too old to be sleeping with ex-Tory ministers, maybe if I was 14 or 15!' he joked, mindful of numerous sexual scandals enveloping the Major Government. A *Melody Maker* journalist was next to Billy – having been granted the interview on the condition that he also slept rough with him.

We burned candles in paper cups throughout the night as various actual homeless people came to talk to us. There were the usual sad tales of a youth who'd been in care since the age of two, a man called Bob who'd emerged from hospital to find his rented room emptied and a cheery silver-haired Scouser who had been thrown out by his wife for drinking and was now telling us jokes in the manner of a stand-up comedian.

At midnight, Derek Nimmo arrived in bow tie and dinner jacket. Oh, golly gosh. Thankfully, he changed into casual gear before taking his place in his box. A 16-year-old boy told us that he used to be a rent boy. 'What's a rent boy?' asked one of the unworldly Australian organisers of the event.

'It's me!' I was tempted to reply. 'Does anyone know how to get a mortgage?'

The weather remained fine and the pillows and boxes we had been supplied with made the night much more pleasant than my previous rough-sleeping experience at St Martins-in-the-Field. Even so, most of the celebrities looked wrecked. Bizarrely, Jeremy Irons and Janet Suzman both donned shades when they woke up at 5.30 a.m. My photographer friend Dave Kampfner began to take pictures of the famous faces and started saying things like 'Cardboard boxes are too formal, we want something more desolate.' Mercifully, the snapper from *The Guardian* kept away from me this time, so the paper avoided creating an entire picture library of Pete May, rough sleeper.

While we were emerging from our boxes, homeless Bob walked past. Suddenly his body gave a series of quivers and jerks and he fell on his face with the sickening thud of flesh on pavement slabs. He was having an epileptic fit. The organisers and police rushed to his aid, but for us middle-class dossers it was a striking illustration of the dangers of sleeping on the streets of London.

The lorries and commuters started to move down Victoria Street and it felt like a separate world. I walked past the Army and Navy store and on to the Peabody flats, and planned to sleep until noon; when I woke up it was 6.30 p.m.

Meanwhile, back in the short-life world, my evenings with Joanne were deteriorating into meaningful discussions about relationships. At least it amused her when I failed abjectly as a rock climber on some Swansea cliffs because of my acute vertigo. She was having doubts about whether she wanted coupledom; while, like most men, I was probably commitment phobic and unsure if I wanted to be a stepdad to two children. And with her ex-partner living in her house, it felt like I was in a relationship with two people: Joanne *and* Eric.

All my relationships seem strangely entwined with my abject failure in the world of property. One Saturday in August, I managed to lock myself out of the Peabody flat. The caretaker opened the door with a chisel, only slightly damaging the door frame. Later that day, I phoned Joanne and we argued about childcare during a holiday she planned to take. We had been having problems ever since a failed holiday in Skye and now our relationship was over.

Six months after she had given up on me, she gave up on London and moved back to her native Swansea, where houses were cheap and the beaches expansive. We were later to become friends again and her children still occasionally see 'Pizza'.

By September, the housing association announced that we were likely to have to hand back the flats by November. Bastards. Peabody must have been the only housing association in the world that could get its builders to turn up on time.

Still, at least the Bank of England was claiming that the worst of the recession was over and Bryan Adams and his '(Everything I Do) I Do It For You' surely couldn't remain at number one forever, could they?

As my worries about another enforced move increased, I was surprised to discover a fellow advocate of affordable housing in Prime Minister John Major. Many of my days were being spent at Lambeth Council offices searching through old microfilm copies of the council's minutes in preparation for a feature in *ROOF*. Major had been a councillor in Lambeth and in 1970 was chair of housing. Back then, he had committed the council to building 2,000 new homes a year by 1974. He'd voted for the building of the now rundown Stockwell Park and Barrier Block estates on Coldharbour Lane, and even recommended, at the height of the Cold War, that two councillors be sent to Poland to study council-house building.

Most hilariously, in true jobsworth style, he'd even forced council tenants who had painted their doors to repaint them back to their original colour. 'Unfortunately, the tenants didn't consult the council before they painted the stonework around their front doors, so they were asked to remove it,' he had told a council meeting in 1970. This information was taken up by the *Sunday Mirror*, which even published an editorial and feature on the 'Two-face Disgrace of Major'.

A few weeks after I'd split up with Joanne, another woman entered my life, a published poet and arts administrator called Camilla. It was starting to be a good decade. We'd been introduced at a party above the Slug and Lettuce in Upper Street, Islington. Her marriage had recently broken up and she only had one child, a four-year-old daughter, who was looked after half the time by her ex-husband. It all sounded quite straightforward after my recent experiences in Brixton.

What really struck me as providential was that Camilla also had a short-life housing flat in west London. Her place in a block belonging to another housing trust was almost identical to mine. The same sturdy brick walls, the same courtyards and sense of solid housing for the deserving poor writer. Here was a woman who would understand the life of a 30-something perpetual rent boy always in fear of receiving 28 days' notice to quit.

For a week, it was great. She'd lived in Essex, liked Joy Division and The Jam, and claimed a pre-Nick Hornby interest in football. I even managed to get her into a Billy Bragg concert at the Town and Country Club through the personal intervention of Billy himself outside the stage door. She should have been impressed. It wasn't long, though, before there were doubts and I was hearing about how she didn't want total emotional intimacy. She had just come out of a marriage split but, even so, back then it seemed London was full of women who wanted to talk about relationships rather than have them. We were destined for a short-life romance.

The recession wasn't over either. By the end of the year, European interest rates were increasing, housing repossessions, bankruptcies and unemployment were rising, while output, consumer confidence and exports were all falling. Each month, the Halifax Building Society would publish some hopeful survey suggesting that the property market had turned and prices would soon be rising again, but they never did.

Terry Waite was finally released that November after nearly five years of captivity as a hostage in Lebanon. It seemed that after a mere 11 months, I was about to be released back into open society, too. Thankfully, with a couple of weeks to go until eviction, the housing association found me a new short-life flat in Elephant and Castle.

Once more it was back to the familiar routine of packing LPs into battered old boxes, dealing with a plethora of hi-fi wires tangled behind the wilting black Habitat unit, wondering if it was worth moving that bad-taste brown sofa and how to take the pine bed apart. Very soon a Thatcherite man with a white van was recruited from the local paper to transport everything I owned across London once more. Would it ever be over? Once again, I was to resume my wanderings in time and space.

ESCAPE TO VICTORIA

MORTGAGE PROSPECTS: Recession has brought some hope to the applicant with falling house prices. However, it must also be noted that several magazines have closed or reduced their budgets and the applicant's income is diminishing. His lack of ability to sustain a long-term relationship with a salaried partner is especially worrying. We suggest he gives up employment as a journalist and moves into a more profitable sector of the economy, such as the repossession business.

AVERAGE HOUSE PRICE IN GREATER LONDON: £83,109

11. The Elephant Man

Peabody Estate, Elephant and Castle, London SE1
November 1991 to May 1994

Elephant and Castle. People drove round it, they queued for buses there and changed Tubes. But now this was my new home – the East Berlin of south London. A land of brutal office blocks, urine-tainted subways and a pink shopping centre that, had Graham Norton been around, would have spawned a thousand camp eulogies.

It was on 14 November 1991 that I became the Elephant Man. The flat was spacious and, although bare, met all my needs; the area itself was extraordinary.

A hint of the Elephant's enticing ambience could be had from my kitchen window: a scenic view of the hollow-windowed shell of what was once the Royal Eye Hospital; whole walls were missing and you could peer into the rooms as if it were a vast grime-covered doll's house. This was bordered by rubble, a makeshift waste-ground car park and a disused pub. It seemed that no one had even bothered to demolish it properly. If it had been 1977 and the first Clash album was on my turntable, then it would have been a perfect punk vista.

By the ruined Eye Hospital stood the roundabout known as St George's Circus. It was here that Dickens' David Copperfield had his bag stolen – Elephant and Castle was dodgy even then.

A short walk along London Road led to the Bakerloo Line station and Elephant proper. Next to the station, those in the ever-present

143

queue for the 184 bus to Camberwell would relieve their tedium by watching cars shunt into each other at London's busiest roundabout. To cross over, pedestrians had to descend into the Elephant underworld and grope their way through a series of dimly lit subways.

Several of these were shut and the others had been refurbished by Southwark Council – amid the neon-lit underground urinals were murals. Garish red, yellow, black, pink, purple, white, grey and brown tiles assaulted the senses before the pedestrian, somewhat disturbingly, discovered that the Great Barrier Reef had been transported to the Elephant. Never has a mosaic been more incongruous. The underground walkway then led to a T-junction permanently patrolled by shifts of persistent beggars.

Here there was a brief shaft of light – like in some Pharaoh's pyramid, touched by the midsummer solstice sun once every year – where the adventurous walker could surface onto the middle of the roundabout and gaze at London's most mysterious structure. Was it a spaceship from *Doctor Who*? On a withered grass surface stood a giant oblong formation, covered in 728 reflective silver squares and cradled by a canopy of black girders. It looked eminently capable of housing a Sontaran, which was probably already conducting fiendish experiments on the Old Kent Road regulars before preparing for one final battle with the Doctor.

After another subterranean brush with beggars and the pervading whiff of ultraviolence, the bemused newcomer arrived at the shopping centre. It wasn't the terrible '60s design of monolithic concrete that shocked, or the fact that an ugly cube known as Hannibal House had been plonked on top to house the Department of Health. No, it was the fact that it was bright pink. Ugliness was to be outfaced by garishness. When it was built in 1965, the Elephant and Castle shopping centre was the first purpose-built shopping mall in Britain.

In 1991, there was still something gloriously '60s about the place (even if it was *Clockwork Orange* chic) with its gleaming tiled floors, 'muzak', escalators and hopelessly optimistic names such as the New Kent Hall and Walworth Gallery.

THE ELEPHANT MAN

It would have been no surprise to find Alex and his droogs, clad in white boiler suits and bowler hats, emerging from the Gold Medal Grill. This was an establishment where smoking seemed to be compulsory, the burger menus were laminated and tea came with the bag still in the cup. It was like entering a '60s Wimpy bar; here, healthy eating was only having three sugars in your tea.

There was still a Woolworths on the ground floor and the sad, half-deserted first-floor level even had a 'unisex' hair salon. The '60s-style lettering on Sensations clothes shop looked like it had been there since, well, the '60s. Tesco seemed to double as the Mike Leigh casting agency, with kids who all looked like Dennis Wise's kid brothers hanging around very large people wearing 'work is the curse of the drinking classes' T-shirts. Elsewhere on the lower level you could find a branch of WH Smith, carpet shops, some cheap hardware stores and a few stalls selling garish paintings that looked like the props department had designed them for Del Boy and Rodders. Up on the third floor, vomit-inducing Technicolor carpets enticed you into the London Palace Bingo Club and ten-pin bowling at the Elephant and Castle Superbowl (possibly the only time 'Elephant' and 'super' have ever been used in the same sentence).

Poor old Southwark Council had attempted to revive the shopping centre with an outdoor market in the concrete trenches and forlorn grey gullies near the cash point, but you suspected that even Scotty from *Star Trek* with a full set of dilithium crystals would have struggled to regenerate Elephant.

By the main entrance, there stood a sad-looking model of a pink elephant with a castle on its back. It was stuck on a plinth above a horrendous pub called the Newington Butts.

Even the area's name was probably a mistake: one theory is that the Elephant and Castle pub was named after England's prospective queen, Infanta de Castile, after James I tried to arrange a marriage between the future Charles I and the Infanta Maria, daughter of Philip III, in 1623. The scheme failed after Charles visited Madrid and presumably decided that the Infanta looked too much like Kathy Burke for his liking. By this time, though, the pub was stuck with its new name. Then, as now, the locals didn't trust this dodgy foreign vernacular and it was rapidly mistranslated into the Elephant and Castle.

Whatever the truth of that tale, the '60s planners wanted their model elephant on display and here it was, surveying the lines of disgruntled, impatient customers by the Abbey National cash dispenser and another huge queue for the bus. By the bus stop, there stood a large box-like building that housed the Northern Line station and looked like a public urinal. Further inspection indicated that part of this structure was indeed a public urinal, which probably explained the confusion among London Underground's customers, many of whom seemed to use the lifts and stairs for bladder sports.

In the local library, it was possible to look up the architect's vision of the gleaming new wonder-mall. Back in 1965, it had seemed like a good idea; the London County Council boasted of the scheme as 'being quite outstanding in its original conception of an arcaded multi-level shopping centre and also producing a simple and extremely fine architectural composition'. The designers probably thought that all the beggars in the urine-tainted subways would be living on lunar colonies by 1991.

Beyond the shopping centre, the environs of the roundabout housed further monstrosities, such as Alexander Fleming House, a kind of multi-storey car park with windows, and the former headquarters of the Department of Health and Social Security (DHSS). But even the DHSS, not an organisation noted for its aesthetic sensibilities, had fled, leaving the building home only to somnolent security guards. At the start of the Old Kent Road, a series of monolithic Stalinist council blocks looked too scary even for a man used to short-life housing to explore.

A few days into my life as the Elephant Man, I went for a drink with Ronald, who was now living in a housing association place in Brixton. As we walked to the pub, our first sight was of a man being chased by a frenzied figure holding an axe. Just another day in south London, we figured.

Yet after a few days in my new environs, I started to love the Elephant. There was the adrenalin-rush of emerging from the

Abbey National cash point unscathed and the unexpected kitsch value of the pink shopping centre. At weekends, Blackfriars Road was eerily silent and it hardly seemed like London at all. Elephant was also extremely close to central London and logic suggested that it was a prime target for gentrification. A short walk down Waterloo Road and you were over the bridge and on the Strand. There was a decent curry house near my flat and it was always possible to get a seat, even on a Saturday night. The local pubs had about five people in them, most of whom looked like gangsters, but after a short walk down Borough High Street, there were fine old pubs like the George and a pleasingly Dickensian aura among the older buildings. You could even go beachcombing on the grey pebbles of the Thames at low tide; or look across to the site of the boot-blacking factory in which Charles Dickens (like myself, a rent boy for much of his early life) was horrified to find himself employed as a child labourer.

My short-life flat on the Peabody estate was fine, too. It had sturdy walls that allowed no noise pollution from my neighbours. The gas fire in the living room worked. It didn't even need decorating and the kitchen was south-facing, pleasingly sunny and large enough to accommodate a Formica-topped table and chairs. Inside the courtyard of the estate, it was relatively quiet and the combination of mainly old people and a few short-lifers worked well.

I began to furnish the flat. All along the London Road, precarious edifices made from office desks and chairs almost obscured a series of second-hand furniture shops. Attempting to purchase a wardrobe, I soon learned that the Elephant was a cash-only society. Foolishly, I had offered to pay by cheque. 'NAAAH! SECON-AN-DEEEELA!' hollered the proprietor, as if I was the stupidest man in the postal district of SE1. At least his stock was cheap, if nasty. 'Look, mate, it's just a plonky old wardrobe. Five pounds to you!' declared the dealer as I hobbled away with an imitation teak, aesthetically horrible, but just-about-effective receptacle for my clothes.

My tenuous relationship with Camilla was still just about happening. She worked in the nearby South Bank Arts Complex and on my first night in my new flat, she phoned and suggested that she visit me after she had finished work. Result, was my initial thought, even if I was receiving more mixed messages than a partially sighted person at a semaphore convention. Perhaps I should have devoted myself to some easier task than trying to understand women – like unravelling the mysteries of DNA.

A day of shifting endless boxes of books and LPs up two sets of stairs was not conducive to sexual athleticism. While my body felt like it had run a marathon twice over and then been asked to turn out in the perpetually overworked West Ham defence, my thoughts turned to children. What would a kid be called who was fathered at the end of a period of physical and mental exhaustion after shifting endless boxes on yet another bloody move around London? Something like Perry Patetic perhaps? But the important thing was that Camilla was here. Maybe she wanted to be the Elephant Woman after all.

At the age of 32, I had met the person you were supposed to meet. Camilla lived in a short-life housing association flat like myself. She was 29 and understood that some us had fallen off the housing ladder. She liked Billy Bragg. She was a writer and prized words. She even claimed to be a West Ham supporter. We went to see *Terminator 2* together. She possessed a copy of *Where's Captain Kirk?* by Spizz Energy.

But a few days later, Camilla still had doubts. Huge doubts. Doubts bigger than the monument on St George's Circus. Doubts bigger than the entire South Bank complex. She explained that she hadn't been out with anyone since she'd split from her husband. It had all happened too quickly, she said. She just wasn't sure she was ready for this. She needed some space. There was something missing. She couldn't offer me what I wanted. There was a sense of detachment.

Being a bloke I couldn't see the problem. If we fancied each other, then why didn't we just get on with it and see what happened? Still, maybe that's why she was a poet and I wasn't.

Camilla was being honest. She kept insisting that there was a problem, but I chose not to listen. There were times when we'd agree not to see each other for two weeks then Camilla would phone me and we'd talk for two hours. Or we'd agree that we were not going out with each other then arrange to meet just as friends and share a bottle of red wine and then end up being somewhat over-friendly and start the whole mess over again.

Generally, our conversations went something like that wonderful scene in Woody Allen's *Bananas* where Louise Lasser bamboozles Woody with a meaningful conversation all about receiving and giving and giving and receiving and not being ready to receive or give or give or receive.

She was airing her doubts on the roundabout. We both agreed that this would make a great first line for a Billy Bragg song, as we spent an hour in the early morning drizzle drunkenly debating the merits of our relationship by the Waterloo Bullring. Taxis stopped to offer us a ride, but we declined. Other cars just shouted abuse. Her doubts were even more complicated than John Major's negotiating postures over the Maastricht Treaty. Eventually, she caught a taxi home.

A few weeks later, I was playing my new video of 'Genesis of the Daleks' when Camilla phoned. She said that she'd met a man from the BBC about whom she had no doubts. No doubts! Despite all her previous honesty, I felt stunned. Hell, I'd even got her into a Billy Bragg concert for nothing and introduced her to the man himself. Did an audience with St William count for nothing?

Camilla is now a successful writer and so she deserves to be. Although it still seems incredible that she could turn down a man with a West Ham season ticket and short-life gaff in Elephant. It was probably best that it ended the way it did though; otherwise we'd still be on that roundabout.

To make it even more painful, she'd phoned during the best-ever *Doctor Who* episode. For years afterwards, I couldn't play it without reminiscing about being dumped just before the really good bit when Davros exterminates the renegade scientists, only to be exterminated himself by a Dalek that doesn't understand the meaning of the word 'pity' because it's not registered in its vocabulary bank.

Camilla wanted to remain friends and said that I would find someone. Only I had found someone, that was the point, and she'd buggered off. Plagued by jealousy, I imagined my TV rival's life, some smooth, successful meeja type free of the murky world of short-life housing, comfortably ensconced in a huge gaff in somewhere like Hampstead having never been given 28 days' notice to quit in his life. But overall, I took it really well – and fled to Australia.

For a while my world imploded. The day after I was dumped, I could hardly drag myself from my poet-free bed to watch West Ham play Wimbledon. We could only draw 1–1 and there were huge on-the-pitch protests against the Hammers bond scheme. We were heading for relegation and it seemed to sum up just about everything.

My recently purchased CD player, which was supposed to play these wonderful, new, utterly indestructible CDs that you could drag behind a lorry and then stamp on and put down a waste disposal chute and still play perfectly, started to jump. On the way to subbing shifts at *Time Out*, I'd walk across Waterloo Bridge looking across to the South Bank, with Billy Bragg's lyrics reverberating through my head.

By February 1992, I'd booked a flight to Australia. Ever since my first trip to Oz in 1989, I'd planned to visit the place again. Now rejection had given me renewed impetus. There wasn't much to stay for in England. Unemployment had just reached two and a half million and even John Major was forced to admit that his Government had underestimated the length of the recession.

The problem of how to keep my flat was soon resolved. My friend Nikki, a Kiwi designer on *Ms London*, was going to move in during my absence and pay the rent. Nikki later recruited Tim Southwell (soon-to-be assistant editor at *Loaded*) to rent the second bedroom. From her letters, it seemed that he was refining the *Loaded* lifestyle with some success in my flat. Perhaps one day there will be a blue plaque on the bedposts.

Australia was a glorious liberation after London. My sojourn took in Perth, Sydney, Canberra, Brisbane and Cairns, with a month in

THE ELEPHANT MAN

New Zealand marvelling at the likes of Doubtful Sound, which may well have been named after Camilla. There were no deadlines there and everyone seemed to have huge houses for half the price of those in London. The Conservatives had inexplicably won yet another general election in my absence, but I was getting used to it by then.

A brief liaison in Sydney helped my self-esteem, but more importantly I made some lasting friends. Half of England seemed to be in Sydney. Every Pom I met was escaping just about everything that was wrong with British life. Again, it was liberating to discover you didn't need all those possessions sitting at home. You could live out of a backpack. What was really necessary? Two pairs of trousers, two shirts, a good book and an inquiring mind.

That trip ended up taking six months. On my return to London, I took another trip, visiting friends in San Francisco for two weeks in the autumn. It was an invigorating year in travel (no one ever called it tourism) terms. By the end of it, I must have been close to wearing drawstring trousers – the true sign of all inveterate travel bores – and writing Lonely Planet guides. The only problem was that although my heart felt much better, I had blown some £7,000 or so on my journeys – money that was meant to be used for a deposit on a flat.

Life in London soon returned to its busy working routine. By the start of 1993, my career was going well: there were regular shifts on *Time Out* and I was recruited to do the Sidelines gossip column for two weeks – the job lasted for nine years. Yes, I was a short-life Nigel Dempster. Much of the job seemed to be going to launches in NCP car parks hoping for a glimpse of Pulp's Jarvis Cocker at some publicity scam organised by Mark Borkowski PR. There was plenty of free beer on hand too, so it was a position I could just about handle. My other activities included subbing for two days a week on the *New Statesman*, writing regularly for *Midweek* and getting the odd piece in *The Guardian*. Was now the time to buy a flat?

Unbelievably, the recession was still dragging on and property prices continued to fall for the first time since the war. Pete May, however, was to property speculation what John Major was to Cabinet unity.

Strangely enough, my speeches to building societies of 'Listen, mate, I met this unobtainable poet and then blew my deposit on a trip to Australia and a single bloke can't possibly afford a flat in London particularly if he's self-employed because you bastards will only give him three times his profit which is always on the low side after my tax-deductible expenses and what I really need is a partner to buy with and are there any tasty birds in your office looking for the Billy Bragg of journalism minus the dosh and will you lend me some money anyway?' didn't seem to get a result.

I'd leave financial offices cursing the cretins who wouldn't give me a mortgage on my turnover (which was only about £15,000 p.a. in 1994 – adequate to live on but journalism has never been as well paid as the public seem to think) rather than my profit. Still, it was almost certain that I would write a bestseller one day and be fantastically rich and buy a house for cash. One day, I'd put £300,000 in notes on the table before those squirming idiots in pinstripes. If only I could get published.

My parents were not about to set up a trust fund for me. My dad had correctly predicted the property recession, but was still convinced housing was overpriced and that the risks of negative equity were huge. 'If you buy with a mortgage, you won't own your house, the bank will own it,' he'd point out. He still needed his investment income to live off and I'd get my share of his money when he died anyway, he explained cheerfully. He then added that he didn't own a house until his late 50s. And I probably wouldn't own one until my late 70s.

My dad would pour another pint of home brew and point out that houses in Northern Ireland were still very cheap. In a way he was right, of course. London was grossly overpriced compared to many parts of the country, but the fact was that my friends were there and if I was ever to make it as a journalist, I had to be in the capital.

Much of journalism seemed to be about socialising: turning up at the office to hand in your floppy disk or stopping for drinks after work with the editor made a difference. If you wanted to sub-edit at magazines – which was a much more stable source of income than selling freelance features – then you needed to be able to get to those magazines, which were invariably in London. So, cheap gaffs in Ulster would have to wait.

And there were too many other distractions to worry about mortgages. For something incredible had happened. In my early 30s, I had suddenly become attractive to women. Aided by biological alarm clocks set on maximum beep with chimes ringing out louder than those at the beginning of Pink Floyd's 'Time', they just might have been starting to think that a nice guy might make a decent partner, and perhaps father, even if he did live in a short-life flat in Elephant. Or maybe they were just desperate.

A woman called Kate, who I'd been at school with, phoned me up after reading an article of mine in the Saturday *Guardian*. We dated for five months or so. She was a teacher who lived in Brixton, as did my next partner in serial monogamy, Caitlin, a Scottish charity worker. Neither relationship lasted. They both had doubts, as ever, and for all Kate and Caitlin's many merits and very pleasing tendencies, such as their willingness to share my bed, I was still foolishly reminiscing about Camilla and a ruined *Doctor Who* episode. Caitlin decided that there was something missing, as women always do when they want to give you a coded message that you have all the sensual appeal of Les Dawson after a vindaloo. That was enough; I resolved to retire from relationships and spend more time with my VHS collection.

But then Nicola arrived. For two days each week, I was subbing at the *New Statesman* where my old pal from *Midweek*, Steve Platt, was now editor. The magazine was permanently in a financial crisis and the Prime Minister had just decided to sue it for libel. An article had simply pointed out that the rumours that Major was having an affair with a cook at Number 10 were completely untrue, yet still he sued and the very survival of the magazine was threatened. Nicola was coordinating the fundraising campaign. This seemed to involve inviting lots of famous socialists to lunches, a job at which she excelled.

We'd known each other as work colleagues for several months

after our eyes first met across a page proof. We'd discussed some new writer called Nick Hornby a lot and she even feigned an interest in football. But by this time, I wasn't sure that I wanted to be involved with anyone and was resigned to a life of singledom. Finally, I'd cracked what women wanted. If you don't care anymore, they become interested. Nicola phoned me up after watching my firm-but-fair performance at the back for the *New Statesman* versus VSO football match and the rest is her story.

Most importantly, Nicola didn't seem to have any doubts. She seemed to like me for the person that I was, short-life flat and lack of career prospects included. And if she wanted 'a bit of rough', then Elephant was the right place. The fact that she was still recovering from a relationship in the Solomon Islands probably helped. It seemed that I was regarded as a safe pair of trousers. Even when she found a woodlouse and an ancient pair of knickers down the back of my sofa (they must have belonged to the person who'd thrown it out), she didn't walk away.

Nicola owned her own flat in Highbury, which she was renting out, and had recently been living in Hackney. On our first night together, she told me how she planned to move to Oxford to become an environmental writer. She had been to public school and made things happen rather than waiting for them to happen to her – an approach I could learn from.

After our first date, she spent three weeks staying with friends in Yorkshire and then moved to Oxford to live in her friend's mum's house by the River Cherwell. She was also working from home as the part-time director of a charity called Forest Management Foundation (something to do with tree-hugging and sustainable forestry). But something positive had happened. She still visited me in London and I was spending every other weekend in Oxford.

Her background was what posh people refer to as 'upper-middle class' and she joked that impoverished toffs could easily be greens, because they were used to not having any heating in their stately homes. She challenged many of my preconceptions and was endearingly eccentric. On our first journey from London to Oxford, she insisted on carrying a terrapin in a bucket on a seat on the bus.

Sometimes her mouth forgot to censor what her brain was thinking and at some highbrow dinner party she'd suggest that someone's dog should be shot.

She took me to parties where people had titles and didn't know who Gazza was. Then there were the Solomon Islanders. Having worked with VSO there for two years, there seemed to be a permanent supply of Solomon Islanders arriving in London, whom Nicola would ask me to entertain and impress with trips to football matches.

My mind was full of prejudice about the aristocracy from the likes of Elvis Costello and of course Paul Weller's tirade against the 'Eton Rifles'. I agreed with Thomas Paine that titles were but nicknames. But now I discovered that some toffs were twits and others were really quite nice. Even Nicola's dad Angus declined to horsewhip me and admitted that he'd once voted Labour. When we first met he had already been diagnosed as having bowel cancer, but was still leading an active life and welcomed me with many a glass of whisky. He seemed to appreciate my sense of humour, too.

Her family's dog was a bitch called Thatcher. Perhaps The Jam couldn't teach you everything there was to know about British class. Maybe all those really nasty Thatcherites of the '80s were the self-made lower-middle classes rather than the one-nation toffs. Or was I just becoming a short-life snob?

My liaison with Nicola certainly impressed the lads at *Loaded*. Tim Southwell and his mate James Brown had called me into the IPC offices to work on the first issues of the mag. James would often ask in his Yorkshire accent, 'Eh, are you still seeing that posh bird then?' with an admiring tone. Posh totty was to become an enduring fantasy for lads' mags.

Tim Southwell wanted to model *Loaded* on both *Midweek* and the fanzines many of us used to work on: good writing covering anarchic, irreverent and blokeish subjects with plenty of football, music, sex, comedy and drinking articles. It was a good idea but, as with most new launches, it would probably only last a couple of issues.

RENT BOY

While I was splitting my time between *New Statesman*, *Loaded*, *Time Out* and *Midweek*, Nicola was permanently mobile and we were spending long weekends in places like Oxford, Devon, Dinan in France and London. It was all going too well. She stayed, but my flat didn't.

In March 1994, yet another eviction notice arrived on my doorstep. You expected them, but they still hurt. Another upheaval and more panic on how to survive in London. Another housing association that gets its builders in on time. My short-life housing association offered me a new place through a myriad of dank railway arches near Waterloo, but in truth I was short-lifed out. Nicola suggested that I move into her Highbury flat with her lodger, a Kiwi called Brett. He was returning to New Zealand in the summer and Nicola suggested that she would then return to London and we could live together.

For a time I vacillated. Nicola and I had only known each other for five months. My work was tied up with my home and I debated whether I could afford to lose my home if my relationship failed. But Nicola was staying in Oxford for another six months so at least Highbury was a way out; and if our relationship flourished then we had a flat together. After twelve and a half years of renting in London, maybe there would at last be some level of security in my home life.

It was time to banish all rushes of commitment phobia and move into the private sector, both in terms of rented accommodation and relationships. At 33, maybe I was finally escaping from my life as a rent boy: moving from a pink shopping centre with the whiff of ultraviolence to a north London land full of cappuccinos and croissants. Pete May had met a posh bird who not only owned a flat but also had a trust fund. For the moment, I would carry on sleeping with my landlady. But there was also a sense that our relationship might last and that maybe not today, maybe not tomorrow, but soon and for the rest our lives, we might even buy property together. Only I was soon to discover that those who believe in the mobility of the property market have never heard of the word subsidence.

THE ELEPHANT MAN

MORTGAGE PROSPECTS: Now is the time the applicant should be buying. However, once again the applicant has been hampered by uneconomic notions of romance and a foolhardy and expensive trip to the Antipodes. He should by now be aware of the building societies' and banks' complete lack of flexibility towards the self-employed and get a sensible job. Or at least a girlfriend with a trust fund. Which we are pleased to see the applicant has finally achieved.

AVERAGE HOUSE PRICE IN GREATER LONDON: £87,443

12. Highbury Fields Forever

Aubert Park, Highbury, London N5
May 1994 to April 2001

Highbury was a land overflowing with delis and candle shops. After Elephant and Castle, the shock of moving to middle-class Georgian and Victorian Highbury was acute. At the age of 33, I had made it to Media City. You knew there was something different about the area because whenever the Arsenal Tube was closed through industrial action, the pavements would be full of bemused TV producers and magazine and national newspaper journalists.

In Aubert Park, our next-door neighbours were an economics correspondent, who could be seen on the BBC's national news every night, and the media editor of *The Guardian*. Clive Anderson was always on Highbury Fields walking his dogs or taking his children to the Oasis Café. Kathy Burke was still on her old manor and half the cast of *EastEnders* were now living in N5.

Nick Hornby would walk the streets like Highbury's patron saint. *Fever Pitch* had proved a publishing phenomenon. You could see him strolling to his office on Highbury Hill or eating out at his favourite Italian restaurant on Blackstock Road. No one bothered him even though he was a hugely successful writer by that stage; he was just one of the local characters. A famous writer in America would have needed 20 minders just to go jogging. The closest thing to a media star that Elephant and Castle had was the man outside the Tube selling the *Standard*.

Then there was the Blair factor. Tony and Cherie Blair were Islington's most famous residents, living just off Upper Street in Richmond Crescent. Blair and Gordon Brown had famously sealed their Granita Pact at a restaurant of the same name on Upper Street. The new leader of the Labour Party came to epitomise the 'Islington chattering classes' to journalists on the *Telegraph* and *Daily Mail*. When Blair listed his favourite recipe as pasta with sun-dried tomatoes, the cliché was complete.

Roger, our local newsagent, insisted that Tony Blair had once lived in Stavordale Road, in one of those roaming three-storey houses beloved of lefty barristers. You suspected that there was probably a Tony Blair story in every part of Islington: no doubt he said 'trust me' in every deli whenever they noticed the expiry date on his cheque guarantee card had passed; when walking his kids on Highbury Fields, he was (to repeat a very old joke) tough on grime and tough on the causes of grime.

Islington was once seen as a rough part of London and it is still a remarkable mix of affluence and poverty. But after Highbury and Islington Tube station opened in the early 1970s, it had become fashionable for the middle classes. The postcodes N1, N4, N5 and N7 were full of Georgian squares and Victorian houses waiting to be gentrified. The barristers, City types and media people were moving in. Property prices had soared in the 1980s and were still high. Every building on Upper Street that wasn't selling food or candles was an estate agent.

The backstreets around Upper Street and Essex Road still concealed council estates where there was real poverty. Gangs of kids would knock cyclists off their bikes and steal their bags in the manner of marauding gangs of Afghan bandits. Around Highbury, the residents of the council estates were friendlier, and new and old Highburyites seemed to mingle without too much conflict – which is why deli could live happily next door to greasy spoon caff on Highbury Barn. In a way, part of Islington's attraction was that it was not yet like Kensington: full of rich people and no one else.

Safe from the threat of eviction at 28 days' notice, it was time to explore my environs. Immediately impressive was the fact that it didn't have mere parks, but an ecology centre, where silver birches grew and moorhens thrived on a pond set upon reclaimed railway land.

If you walked up Aubert Park and onto Blackstock Road, it soon became Highbury Barn, a road with a busy parade of thriving local shops and the Highbury Barn pub. The rest of Highbury was so genteel that it didn't seem to have any other pubs. People held dinner parties or dined in the myriad restaurants on Upper Street. My London folk memory could vaguely remember one pub somewhere just off Highbury Fields, but it had long since been refurbished and gentrified into designer flats for Apple Mac artisans.

Not much had changed since 1869. From 1740 onwards, Highbury Barn (named after the dairy barn on the site) had developed as a five-acre pleasure garden. Starting off as a cake-and-ale house (and back then these really would have been organic), it acquired a bowling green and tearooms. Then the Barn was equipped as a 'great room' which could seat 3,000 diners.

In the 1850s, the Barn was converted into a concert hall and Archibald Linton built the Leviathan Platform, a 400-foot-square open-air dancing platform, which he no doubt thought might at least get him onto the front cover of *Time Out*. It was a bit like the modern Highbury stadium with early floodlights; the Leviathan was illuminated by gas globes and featured an in-house orchestra.

In 1865, Highbury's first fringe theatre and alternative comedy club emerged when the Alexandra Theatre was reconstructed on the site. Proprietor Edward Giovanelli, a former clown and early Ben Elton figure, performed comedy and pantomime with his wife, and engaged tightrope walkers, Siamese twins, music hall artistes and no doubt a couple of feminist acts doing jokes about tampons.

But the new inhabitants of the terraces being built all over Highbury soon complained that the crowds from the Barn were disturbing their dinner parties with their rowdiness, immorality and 'horseplay'. A riot in 1869 resulted in Giovanelli losing his licence and peace was restored for the readers of the Victorian *Guardian*. By 1883, most of the Barn grounds had been developed, although the Highbury Barn pub is still on part of the original site.

The spiritual epicentre of modern Highbury appeared to be the Da Mario deli. In Elephant, you were thankful to find white sliced bread and tomato ketchup at Tesco. In Highbury, there was a constant queue of Tony and Cherie lookalikes demanding humous, apple-smoked cheddar, Parma ham, virgin olive oil, ciabatta, walnut bread, and marinated mushrooms and olives. The chattering and chartering classes besieged Da Mario seven days a week until it closed at 9 p.m. My first visit there set the pattern for the next ten years, and resulted in an encounter with a pal of Nicola's who was a news producer for Channel 4. More deals and projects were probably finalised at the Da Mario deli than the Groucho Club.

Next to Da Mario was a specialised cheese shop called La Fromagerie selling succulent semi-liquid brie and just about every other cheese imaginable, plus croissants, olive and rosemary bread, mini quiches, organic sea salt, organic chocolates and marinated digits de customer after I paid my first bill.

A fish and chip shop stood by the Highbury Barn pub, but even the chippies were different up north. The woman serving me announced that she had a friend who worked for *The Guardian*. When she didn't have any change from my £5, she suggested that I could pay her the next time I was passing. In the cash-only economy of Elephant, such trust was unheard of. Asking for credit would not only have offended, but probably resulted in your dismembered body being found in several suitcases on the grey pebbles on the Thames foreshore at low tide.

Highbury Fields was an expanse of green park between Highbury Barn and Highbury and Islington station. The Fields were surrounded by Georgian houses worth a million each. Squirrels bounded up horse chestnut trees and at night the imitation gas lamps flickered evocatively above the odd mobile phone thief loitering in the bushes.

The recycling bins by the swimming pool on Highbury Fields were astonishing. In Elephant, you would have been lucky to find a dead dog and the contents of someone's dustbin. But here, the paper and bottle banks were overflowing. The council appeared to have lost all control of its burgeoning glass, aluminium and paper mountains. Piles of cans, bottles and newspapers lay by the over-nourished bins. Cars regularly punctured their tyres on the shards of broken glass in the road. All day and all night there was the never-ending clinking of glass. An endless parade of Highbury mums with young children safely strapped in car seats could be seen lugging huge piles of papers from out of the back of their hatchbacks and estates. In fact, the recycling bank contained nothing but *Observers* and *Guardians*, and maybe the odd *Independent* or *FT*. When a stray copy of *The Mirror* or *The Sun* slipped out of my bag, it felt a bit like I'd been caught with a copy of *Penthouse*.

Even the swimming pool on Highbury Fields was decidedly middle class. Instead of south London 'musak', they played Otis Redding for career mums as they swam off the previous night's rocket salad. By the pool stood the public loo where gay playwright Joe Orton had been cottaging. There's also a plaque commemorating Britain's first gay rights demonstration there in 1970.

Once you had crossed Highbury Fields you came to the start of Upper Street. There was no food to be bought here – apart from in restaurants – only, as a friend of mine once put it, 'lots of shops selling useless things'.

The Gill Wing shop seemed to specialise in Islington-person paraphernalia. If teapots shaped as cats, a cactus or a Marshall amplifier were your thing, then here was the place to get them, along with wooden pieces of fruit, buckets, designer milk churns, a Sarah Crozier hat kit with designer pin, vases, imitation classic-valve radios, Neal's Yard rosewater, Neal's Yard calendula shampoo, multi-coloured flower pots and American gum machines (with refill balls).

Next door, another Gill Wing shop specialised in natural sandals – what else in such a liberal borough as Islington? A helpful sign read: 'Sandals are the perfect way to rehabilitate abused feet.' I couldn't think of a better way of getting abused feet than by walking down the Old Kent Road in sandals.

The third shop of the triumvirate was the Gill Wing cook shop, full of designer blue-and-white hooped mugs for a fiver each, reproductions of old-fashioned glass bottles, Bodum cafetières, woks, olives, virgin olive oil, herb vinegar and three-year-old balsamic vinegar. The ubiquitous Gill Wing seemed to be taking over Islington. On Highbury Corner, her café, imaginatively entitled Le Café, was the place for Islington bohos to peruse the Sunday papers over cappuccino while flaunting their programmes from the ecologically sound Schumacher Awards ceremony.

Even the fast food was upmarket. Never mind *The Sun* and *The Mirror*. A little further down Upper Street in Generous George's Subs sandwich shop, copies of the *Independent*, *NME*, *Big Issue* and *The Islingtonian* were on the counter for the perusal of customers.

On the wall was a 'customer's newsletter'. It said that a former employee called Dave was now planning to set up an organic farm in Hertfordshire. It also revealed that Kathy Burke was a regular and that Generous George's six-foot submarine-shaped sandwiches were going down really well at kids' parties (no one in Islington ever had children, just kids). What would a customer newsletter in Elephant have said? No doubt something like: 'Chief fryer Dave has left because he's been banged up and our chips are proving a great success with the homeless in the Waterloo Bullring.'

Even the Bagel Diner was accommodating a woman in a beret with cropped hair and steel-framed glasses sitting at the table with a cup of herb tea, Filofax open, writing copious notes on a large notepad. A man with a goatee beard and a woman in tartan trousers were sitting opposite a woman in a lumberjack shirt accompanied by a friend in what appeared to be a fisherman's smock.

Then there was Islington's burgeoning ethnic chic industry. All over Islington, flats – including my own – were being transformed into mini versions of the African bush. A shop called Shumba sold scary Zimbabwean tribal masks, tribal salad spoons, 'Mandela Rules' baskets, model rhinoceroses, giraffes and elephants all 'made from dead wood by skilled Zimbabwean craftsmen'. Aarong sold Bangladeshi rugs, baskets, robes and model elephants. Nearer the Angel, Alternative East was flogging Mayan rainsticks for £29 each, Mayan music balls and Indian chests. I wasn't exactly sure what Mayan music balls were, but they seemed to be a pretty essential purchase in N1.

And, of course, there had to be the Oddball Juggling Company. In the early 1990s, the terminally trendy had taken on juggling as a form of executive stress relief. Middle managers were becoming fixated with jester chic. Even whilst on holiday, health service managers would get out their balls and begin throwing them up in the air, relieving their own stresses by quadrupling them in others.

Other typical Islington shops included the Upper Street Bookshop with used copies of Ezra Pound and James Joyce's *Ulysses* in the window; a second-hand designer clothes shop called Secondo Mano; Paradox, selling Junior Gaultier, Jasper Conran and Nicole Farhi; a stripped-pine shop called At The Sign of the Chest of Drawers; and Rebecca Street selling a knock-down £1,125 dress at just £950. I felt both mentally bankrupt and exhausted after just one trip.

But the main difference for a former Elephant Man was the endless array of restaurants. Here there were Vietnamese, Thai, Malayan, Singaporean, Mexican, American, Lebanese, Indian, Italian, Turkish and Chinese eateries within a few hundred yards of each other. Even the Upper Street Fish Bar sold oysters and poached halibut with herb sauce.

Was this land, fit for sundried tomatoes and juggling Christian socialists like Tony Blair, even part of London? A sign on Café Flo announced that it was 'ouvert 7 jours'. There were pâtisseries on every corner and after shopping at Sainsbury's you'd find yourself confronted by Le Montmartre café bistro.

Would there be any pubs in this land of Mayan balls? Ronald had now bought a place in Shepherd's Bush, but after a trip up the Victoria Line he joined me once more in our perpetual search for a real local pub.

Upper Street had been colonised by chains and theme bars; it was nothing but the Slug and Lettuce, Finnock and Firkin, Harvey Wallbangers bar, Cuba Libre, Café Rouge and Ruby in the Dust. The Camden Head was better and yielded a sighting of whoever the actress was who played Lisa Duckworth in *Coronation Street* and the King's Head Theatre bar was decent but packed, and had an annoying retro affectation of charging customers in shillings and pence. The Hen and Chickens on Highbury Corner was just a little too trendy and loud.

Eventually, we discovered the Compton, a pub that appeared to have been uprooted from Cornwall and deposited in the backstreets of Canonbury. It served Abbot and IPA but even here there was the resident Islington celebrity – Paul Whitehouse from the Harry Enfield show.

Initially, part of me longed for Elephant's pink shopping centre, restaurants that had menus you could understand and shops that sold baked beans. Could a man exist on a diet of nothing but Zimbabwean tribal masks, Bangladeshi baskets, multi-coloured scented candles and juggling balls? But another part of me was tempted to march down to the recycling bins and sign up for the gym at Highbury pool. And despite the clichés, Da Mario's sundried tomatoes were really pretty good. Within weeks, I was metamorphosing into an Islingtonian.

Nicola's flat was in a late-Victorian house at the lower end of the hill that descends down Aubert Park. The road was named after Alexander Aubert, an insurance broker and amateur astronomer who lived in the now-demolished Highbury House. Back then, you could see the night sky in N5. He built his own observatory there and re-erected the St Peter-Le-Poer clock from Broad Street in the grounds, as you do. Aubert was a busy man. He also commanded the Loyal Islington Volunteers from 1798 to 1801, a group of men who would pelt all rivals to the British Empire with pistachio nuts and olives.

Ignoring the somewhat grimy and decaying grey stair carpet and front door at my new gaff, the property was a rather elegant-looking house that had been hastily converted into flats. Beneath me was a one-bedroom flat inhabited by a man called David, who worked for the government. An active Christian, he had no television and preferred evening prayers to parties, so was as quiet a neighbour as you could find.

On the ground floor were Sharon and Matthew, a couple who were currently on two children but soon to reach four, all somehow crammed into a one-bedroom flat. They were understandably a little noisier than David and periodic hollering from Sharon at Matthew and the kids permeated our lives, particularly in the summer when the garden was augmented with a sandpit, paddling pool and children. It was amazing how they all survived in such a small space. We were later to realise that Sharon and Matthew must have been brilliant parents just to keep the whole family routine functioning in such a minute area.

Inside the double Banham locks on my new flat's front door (bought after a burglary in the 1980s), your first glimpse was of the loo, which, according to the ancient Chinese art of feng shui (which was just becoming big in Islington – a friend of a friend was reputedly earning £400 an hour at it), was very bad and a sign that your wealth would soon be flushed away. Years of renting had done that anyway, so I wasn't too bothered.

The kitchen was smaller than the one at Elephant, but there was a spacious lounge (which I now had to call the living room) and, upstairs, two bedrooms with sloping ceilings – finally I had moved to a writer's garrett. According to my mate's feng shui book, slanting beams, walls and halls were meant to portend strange happenings, while a badly aligned door and small window was surely suppressing the flow of chi through the house. But sod that. Having lived in 12 homes in London so far, I had been inadvertently practising the art of furniture placement for most of my adult years. Leading such a peripatetic existence, I must have experienced every form of good and bad chi going.

In a way, Nicola and I were well suited. She had never thrown anything away in her life. On the corridor wall downstairs, Nicola had hung her collection of ethnic masks. She was one of those people who kept those mask shops in Upper Street thriving. Some of them had even been collected from more distant lands on her eco-trips to the Solomon Islands and PNG (as greens habitually referred to Papua New Guinea). Every mantelpiece was covered in ornaments and heirlooms. It's easy to identify anyone of upper-middle-class pedigree because their stairway walls are always covered with pictures. Nicola had old prints of hounds, horse pictures, framed posters of the Pacific and pictures from college on every available foot of wall.

There were huge mounds of books, boxes of letters dating back to boarding school, overflowing filing cabinets and boxes, suitcases and hatboxes stuffed under the bed and on wardrobes. Plus numerous glass jars full of paper clips and elastic bands and safety pins and badges and floppy discs and staplers. And she hadn't even moved back in yet.

To Nicola's clutter was added my extensive collection of paraphernalia. The plonky £5 wardrobe from Elephant was installed in the bedroom. West Ham programmes, old copies of *Midweek* and the *New Statesman*, *Rothman's Football Yearbook*s and a huge collection of novels. My spare bed, my desk from the National Dairy Council and a bedside cabinet had to be stored in the utility room on the stairs. It was a bit like a scene from the TV series *A Life of Grime*. Whoever invented the concept of decluttering your life was probably inspired by this very flat.

Initially, I was sharing with Brett, a QPR-supporting New Zealander, who was a journalist at IPC. Nicola had bought the place in 1989 and consequently had a relatively low mortgage. While she was living in Oxford, we were both paying her a well-below-market rent and I was getting to sleep with my landlady. It seemed like a result for any rent boy. Brett and myself shared until Christmas 1994 when he returned to New Zealand and then I was to have the flat to myself until Nicola returned to join me the following year.

Our relationship was going well. Just as long as I remembered that upper-middle-class people were obsessed with table manners, thank-you letters and pets, it would all be fine. No wonder Lord Lucan has never been found; he will eventually be given up by his posh chums when he forgets to write a letter saying thank you for his weekend break.

HIGHBURY FIELDS FOREVER

I had regular work, too: a couple of days a week subbing at *New Statesman* and a variety of pseudonyms – I was London Spy on *Midweek* and Sidelines on *Time Out*, while *Loaded* had suddenly started selling half a million copies. Basically, those of us around at the start had just put together a fanzine full of blokeish humour – it just happened to turn into a publishing sensation.

During 1995, I continued to write features and sub at *Loaded* and suddenly everyone was impressed. Here was a whole magazine based on 'word wanking'. After years of listening to feminists declaring that lacy underwear was murder, it was strangely liberating to admit that blokes sometimes liked looking at pictures of women wearing it. And the young women of the '90s, inspired by the early example of Madonna, seemed much less afraid of being seen as both strong and sexual. Yet the magazine created huge outrage. What was considered acceptable for models to wear in *Vogue* was suddenly seen as disgusting by some puritans in the media.

Critics tended to ignore the fact that the early editions of *Loaded* contained some brilliant writing and didn't feature that many pin-ups. It could also make political movements accessible. Martin Deeson wrote the most effective green recruitment feature ever published when he visited the anti-Newbury bypass protesters. He simply wrote about the humour of the protest and the Monty Python jokes rather than the politics and it was brilliant.

The schizophrenic sensation of working at the earnest *New Statesman* one day and puerile but brilliant *Loaded* the next was really rather enjoyable. It was also perhaps significant that many of the lads in the offices had enjoyed similar accommodation disasters. We didn't get where we were today without knowing a squalid gaff when we lived in one. One of the best features *Loaded* ever did was 'Wotcha!', a parody of *Hello!*, in the December 1994 issue. Here 'Mr and Mrs Loaded' invited you into their lovely home. The cover line read 'We lift the lid on modern-day squalor' next to a picture of a dilapidated toilet, plus 'Revealed! The shitholes we call home!'

My experiences at Hermes Point were recounted under the headline 'Dump'. Fellow hack Michael Holden revealed how he'd lived in a place with no TV, radio, carpets, heating or lights in Kilburn High Road, where he was supposed to carry out renovations in lieu of rent. A lost weekend later, after food poisoning, a death threat on the answer machine and severing his foot on exposed carpet rods, he was out, the landlady's giant cousin demolishing the place around him. While Tim Southwell recalled living above a toilet warehouse in Edgware Road, complete with turquoise carpet, porthole window looking out on a brick wall three feet away, plus a growing population of rats and the obligatory paper-thin walls through which he could hear a huge rugby player next door screaming with pain after his jaw had been smashed and then wired together. That *Loaded* feature should have taught me that perhaps decay and Pete May were inseparable bedfellows.

It was in 1995 that the cracks started to appear. Nicola had moved in that summer and, surrounded by our mutual piles of clutter, we were living together quite happily. She was running the Forest Management Foundation from home and returned from Oxford with huge files on sustainable logging that were the width and weight of a piece of illegally felled mahogany. We would eat out at any one of the 3,000 restaurants on Upper Street, visit the theatre and cinema or go away for weekends.

But the flat seemed colder than usual. Large gusts of air were coming in around the sash windows in the living room. Hairline cracks had opened up underneath them and other fractures were appearing all over the house. When you looked up at our windows from the street they were crooked.

I had wanted a woman of substance, only now it seemed I was living with a woman of subsidence. We were suffering from the nemesis of property owners all across London – and I wasn't even a property owner. Still, at least Nicola was insured. Acting with the freeholder of the property, who owned the two flats beneath us, she contacted the insurance company.

The insurers duly sent two men in suits who stuck some studs in the wall around the cracks and, erm, that was it. Six months later they came to look at them again, took a few readings and left. We soon learned that just because a house had huge cracks in it, it did not mean that it had subsidence. There was the London clay to consider and the tree in the road and the cellar and the drainage. Those cracks clearly had to be monitored for movement. Perhaps the title of Oasis's brilliant debut album *Definitely Maybe* had been inspired by the Gallagher brothers' dealings with an insurance company.

A crack was also opening up where our bedroom was attached to the flank wall at the end of the terrace. I had visions of waking up in a three-walled bedroom, several tons of bricks having cascaded onto the parked cars and pedestrians below.

Nicola was keen on a place with a garden and it would have made sense to buy together at this point. At the time, the average price of a London home was still only £89,102. She had even hired a council allotment, such was her desperation to grow her own organic vegetables. The market was still low and you could pick up a huge three-storey house in Stavordale Road, close to our place, for around £200,000. Today, they're worth half a million or more. Yet until Nicola could sell her flat, we were stuck. And there was no chance of selling it until the subsidence was cured.

In the summer of 1995, we visited Nicola's former home in the Solomon Islands. On my 35th birthday, we stayed together in a cave on the island of Bellona. The proprietors, a very friendly couple called John and Nita, had put a double bed in the cave along with a tarpaulin above it to catch any stray drips.

We watched the waves of the Pacific battering the coral. A colony of bats inhabited another nearby cave. Coconut crabs scurried below us and one that was destined for our dinner ran around the cave before John caught it. The following morning, a seagull dropped a poisonous sea snake onto a rock at the entrance to our cave. It made its way into a corner and Nicola was extremely frightened; I wasn't, of course. After a lifetime of flat-sharing in London, I felt I could face anything. No venomous reptile had ever sent me a note telling me to leave or nicked my milk from the fridge.

We returned home and the monitoring went on. The men in suits had started to do verticality surveys, whatever they were. It was clear to even a non-surveyor like myself that our verticality levels were pretty soon going to be horizonticality levels unless someone acted soon.

The fact that our home was going the way of the walls of Jericho sounded about as worrying as our front door needing a new coat of paint in the bland language of the engineers. By June 1996, the loss adjusters had conceded, 'It would appear that the flank wall has rotated slightly away from the main body of the house causing cracking to occur to internal partitions and the load-bearing wall.'

The solution, as ever, was to do just a little bit more monitoring: 'In view of this, we have recommended to insurers that an engineer is appointed to carry out site investigations and report on the level and degree of cracking.'

There was plenty to distract us while the men in black monitored the walls every three months. Penguin had commissioned a book called *The Lad Done Bad* on soccer sleaze, which I was co-writing with Denis Campbell and Andrew Shields. In between writing chapters on Lothario soccer aces, I'd invite the subsidence men up to monitor their stud movements; I felt a little like Miss Flite in *Bleak House*, always hopelessly optimistic about finally receiving a judgement. Whenever the monitoring men visited, they would assure us that a verdict was expected soon. Nicola was increasingly feeling that the uncertainty about her flat was preventing her from progressing with her life.

Nicola had been under huge stress as she watched her father Angus's health deteriorate. A few days before he died, just before Christmas 1996, he managed to fax me a message of good luck for my book launch, a gesture which was much appreciated.

New Labour were elected in May 1997. After watching Billy Bragg live at the Mean Fiddler (why change the habit of more than a decade?), Nicola and I spent the rest of the night watching Portillo lose at our friend Bob's housing association flat in Barnsbury, Islington, the heartland of New Labour. It was an ecstatic night and euphoria seemed to grip everyone on the streets. There would be no more imperialistic wars, no more privatisation, no more sleaze or cronyism; admittedly Blair and Brown had disguised their manifesto in the language of prudence, but we knew there would be radical policies to come now they had been elected.

Property prices in London were still rocketing. Prime Minister Blair sold his Islington house in 1997 for a mere £700,000. At the time it seemed like a great price, but Blair was to see the market soar and his house change hands for more than £1 million a few years later. In May 2004, it was put on the market for £1.69 millon. On television, countless shows like *Changing Rooms* and *Location, Location, Location* dedicated themselves to the British obsession with property. It had the feel of the '80s all over again.

Nicola was working as a freelance journalist as well by that stage, which made our incomes doubly precarious; we were still dependent on selling the flat to put down a big deposit and still trapped in a wobbly property in Highbury. When the flat was valued, it was worth something close to £180,000, but it was an asset that couldn't be realised until the insurers sorted out their verticality levels.

Oasis and Blur were both at the top of the charts and being fêted by Tony Blair, while Jarvis Cocker wanted to be like the 'Common People'. But the real Cool Britannia was in our flat. The cracks around the windows were widening and we had to fit perspex sheets over their frames to try to retain some heat. It got so cold that we discussed having children as a means of creating some body warmth.

It wasn't any warmer when we visited one of Nicola's green friends in North Wales, either. She was paying a very low rent in return for doing some building work on her old farm-worker's cottage. Consequently, we stayed in a house with only half a roof, holes in the window and a compost loo that involved complicated processes with sawdust and tiger worms. For all the ecological merits of compost loos, I rapidly decided that the superb invention of Thomas Crapper was not something I wanted to live without.

Now it's finished and has central heating, that house is just fine, but back then, when our hostess was wearing three pairs of trousers and the green pal sleeping in the hammock was still fully clothed, it became obvious that I just wasn't hardy enough for the sustainable green life several miles from the nearest paper shop. 'I guess we'll always have Powys,' I muttered to Nicola as we shivered beneath two duvets in our thermals.

As soon as Nicola had adopted a cat called Honey, it had been clear that she wanted children. Honey's male owner had been stabbed to death in a squat in Stavordale Road and Nicola had found the little mewing cat outside its former home and immediately adopted it. In a way, Honey was a victim of London's housing crisis too. The police had been knocking at every door but none of us had heard or seen anything. After all, there had been an Arsenal match on that night. A bemused officer remarked, 'What, you're all journalists in this street and no one talks to each other!'

Actually, the murder helped us meet a lot more people in the community. Soon, I was renting Mary's spare bedroom as an office. She was a teacher with two children who lived a few doors down the street and was going through a relationship break-up at the time. On my morning journeys to work, I'd regularly encounter Rose, a lovely elderly lady who was the street's unofficial policewoman and knew everything that was going on. She'd lived in London all her life and I'd regularly hear tales of her rescuing cats from wasted buildings during the Blitz or her cycling trips with her late husband Harry.

One of the great things about living in central London is it's so easy to escape. We enjoyed regular forays from Euston and King's Cross. Over the summer of '97, Nicola and I became walking-class heroes, completing the 190 miles of Alfred Wainwright's coast-to-coast walk from St Bees in Cumbria to Robin Hood's Bay in Yorkshire. Staying in Lake District hotels and Yorkshire Dales bed and breakfasts, we wondered if perhaps an escape to the north of England might one day solve our housing dilemma. While relaxing in Robin Hood's Bay at the end of the walk, we conceived our first daughter. We then conceived two more books: my own tome on Sunday League football, *Sunday Muddy Sunday*, and Nicola's eco-guide to car culture, *The Estate We're In*.

Lola was born in June 1998, just after the books were published. She was tiny, but soon she would be mobile and we wanted her to have a garden one day. At 37, I had become a father and didn't want my daughter to ever discover my shameful past life as a rent boy. She needed a secure home where there was no landlord ready to change the locks.

At this point, Nicola started having doubts – although they were not so much about giving and receiving as about my nappy changing abilities. A month after giving birth, she wrote to the loss adjusters pointing out that now she had a small baby, she was very keen to sell her flat, which had just been valued at £200,000. The person who replied was clearly wasted in property and should have been in the engine room of the USS *Enterprise*.

We learned that 'the precise level survey has not been related to a fixed datum'. There was talk of drainage repairs and a promise that the verticality survey would be forwarded to us just as soon as the dilithium crystals were charged and Mr LaFarge had made it so.

At least becoming a parent allowed me to explore a new side of Highbury and escape the subsidence fiasco. I'd go buggy racing on Highbury Fields with Lola giggling inside as I ran very fast along the paths, ignoring the stares of disapproving mothers. Forget the Groucho; my favourite was the Two O'Clock Club on the Fields, with a brunch of Arancini and chips beforehand at Anna's Oasis Café. Indeed, looking after a child in Highbury was ideal for celebrity-spotting journos. Why, there was Tory MP Boris Johnson playing with his kid in the sandpit and comedian Phil Cornwell at playgroup. And was that Clive Anderson ordering chips with his girls?

Wednesday mornings saw my regular appearances at the playgroup at St Augustine's Church. Often I was the only man there; surrounded by young, often rather attractive mothers, I felt a bit like the John Travolta of the knackered dad generation. It was also a great source of material. Soon my fatherhood experiences were being recycled on the parents' page of *The Guardian*.

While some friends with children were thinking of leaving London for the countryside, it seemed to me that the city was the new country. People in villages had no shops, relied on cars and never met anyone. But here in Highbury, it was just like *The Vicar of Dibley*. Nicola was on countless committees: the Friends of Gillespie

Park committee (the local ecology centre), the management committee of Lola's nursery and the church playgroup rota. She'd also signed up to Growing Communities, an organic vegetable scheme in Stoke Newington. There seemed to be more organic vegetables in Highbury than you'd ever find in the real countryside, where it was just Tesco megastores and prairie fields drenched in pesticides. Each Wednesday, one of us would cycle to the pick-up point and return laden down with re-used plastic bags full of potatoes, onions, cabbage, cauliflower, mushrooms and celeriac. It felt like we were the Richard Briers and Felicity Kendal of N5.

In December 1998, it became apparent why I hadn't yet got on the property ladder – I'd never asked Geoffrey Robinson for a loan. Unfortunately, he'd bought the *New Statesman* just after I'd stopped working for it. At the time in charge of the Millennium Dome, Peter Mandelson was forced to resign that month after it emerged that in 1996 his plush Notting Hill house had been paid for with a £373,000 loan from Robinson, who was then Paymaster General. Geoff was certainly a lot more flexible than my building society.

When Labour were elected, Mandelson had forgotten to mention this loan and its possible conflict of interest to his colleague and boss, Tony Blair. It seemed to sum up the property madness of Britain: that loan could have bought a whole street in the Minister's Hartlepool constituency. After the scandal emerged, the Notting Hill property was hastily sold.

The pair had met at a dinner party and Mandelson claimed that Robinson had suggested the idea of the loan. However, in his memoirs, Robinson later claimed that it was Mandelson who had initiated the idea. Robinson wrote, 'He told me it was a dingy place in a square at the southern end of Islington, close to King's Cross and Farringdon Road.'

It was also a deal that horrified most students of the property market. What was Mandelson doing buying in one of the most expensive areas of London? Surely a real player and political tactician like Mandelson should never have needed a loan. With a little foresight, he could have simply bought a home in an up-and-coming area and dramatically increased the value of his property that way, rather than opting for top-of-the-market Notting Hill. Choosing the fashionable place of the moment showed a worrying lack of imagination. Had he never considered Kensal Rise, Elephant and Castle, Bermondsey with a Tube, Highbury Borders (oh, all right then, Stoke Newington), Hoxton or Dalston?

The tabloids had great fun tracing the 'dingy flat' Mandelson had left behind. From Mandelson's description of it, you imagined the sort of dwelling George Orwell described in *Keep the Aspidistra Flying*. It was in fact a listed Georgian property in fashionable Wilmington Square, Clerkenwell, rather than a damp refuge for a brassic politico.

The two-bedroom flat was photographed in *The Sun* with its high ceilings, chandeliers, original classical cornicing and mahogany floor in the dining room. Mandelson had sold it to a solicitor for £180,000 in 1996 and by the time Robinson published his memoirs in 2000, it was worth £300,000.

It seemed a tale fitting for the new millennium, encapsulating New Labour's move from idealism to materialism. The grandson of former Labour deputy leader Herbert Morrison was simply after a leg up the property ladder like the rest of us. Once ministers like Profumo had been brought down by call girls; now it was loans for homes.

We both liked living in Highbury. Nicola was taking the procrastination over the subsidence work with equanimity, apart from the odd bout of hair-pulling and cries that her mother wouldn't give her any furniture until she'd got a grown-up house and now she was years behind her friends and she wanted to be like Virginia Woolf and have *A Room of One's Own* that wasn't seen through a sinking window and when she was young she wanted to be the head of the UN and look at her now and if only I'd had a flat to sell when I'd met her or my parents had given me some money then we wouldn't be in the situation we were now and anyway why did I never buy the toothpaste?

It could have been worse, I protested. At least we were living in a desirable part of London, albeit in a flat that was suffering a verticality crisis. I might even learn to be a decent cook if we stayed around there much longer. Nigel Slater lived just off the Barn and Jamie Oliver was often spotted in the local butcher's or at La Fromagerie.

One day, we'd be able to sell her flat and we, or rather she, would be loaded. Although we'd missed the bottom of the market in the early '90s, we would be able to move when the subsidence work was done.

Most of 1999 was taken up with the bressummer beam dispute. Where I'd previously have thought a bressummer beam was some sort of headlight on a Swedish car, I discovered that it was in fact the beam above the top of the bay window on the ground floor. Although it was in the freeholder's flat, there was much argument about the fact that it was 'failing in deflection' (i.e. it was crap) and whether it was contributing to the 'downward movement of the brickwork'. It was always strangely reassuring to find the loss adjuster's ever more ingenious ways of describing dirty great cracks and crevices around our *Alice in Wonderland*-like windows.

Progress was almost made in 2000, with talk of underpinning work and tendering. The insurance company very kindly filled some of the worst cracks with ugly white foam, so that it appeared like some alien life form was attempting to seep out of the bowels of our house.

Only then the original engineer was dismissed and a new man appointed who suggested 'strapping' to solve the problem, as if our home were just suffering a hamstring tweak. The old engineer told us that the bellying in the flank wall was far too severe for this to work. All this was compounded by legal disputes over the party wall. We were told that 'a meaningful commencement on site cannot be made until the party wall matters are concluded'. We were not too sure what a 'meaningful commencement on site' was, but we were certainly now experiencing the meaningful commencement of property ennui.

When 2001 arrived it was not as Arthur C. Clarke predicted. There was no computer telling us, 'I'm sorry, Dave, I can't do that.' Instead, it was an insurance company and our finances were spiralling down a black hole, through a parallel universe and back to the origins of all matter before the Big Bang when cracks had first appeared in our walls.

In February 2001, our second daughter Nell was born at home, in the corner of the subsidence-ridden living room. Despite Nicola's contractions, the house remained upright throughout the labour. It seemed that we would sire more generations than at the start of the Old Testament before we would ever leave Aubert Park. It was a fine residence for a couple, a terribly restricting one for anyone with children, for buggies, a two-year-old daughter and baby Nell all had to be coaxed, cajoled and lifted up and down three flights of stairs. The average price of a house in Greater London was soon to hit £188,342. When I'd moved in almost seven years ago, it had been just £87,433. Our only hope of ever buying together was if we could sell Nicola's flat.

And then it was besieged by rodents. They had come up from the ground floor and started popping up from behind the cooker and the washing machine. We tried humane traps, but they were useless. A man who had coped with cockroaches and asbestos, however, could surely beat a few pesky mice. After watching Michael Palin in *Hemingway Adventure*, I decided to adopt the role of small-game hunter, setting six traps with strategic precision around the kitchen, making sure they were out of reach of two-year-old Lola. In a couple of weeks, 13 mice were dead.

Each morning I found myself checking and baiting my traps and then disposing of the bodies in the undergrowth at the Islington ecology centre. I wondered about following Palin's example and donning a 340 Bush Poplin (it was Hemingway's favourite safari jacket). It would, after all, be just the gear for my Highbury killing grounds, containing 'a shell pocket, recoil pad, working epaulettes with box stitching, two expandable chest pockets, two huge bellowed cargo pockets for shells and a sleeve pocket for shooting glasses'. All it lacked was a box-stitched cheese pocket and customised mouse-trap holder.

Apart from our furry visitors, we were alone, the other tenants having moved out. David below us had moved to a new rented flat on City Road. Sharon and Matthew and their four kids in the ground-floor flat had been re-housed by a Clapton housing association after part of their sodden ceiling collapsed. Water had been gathering on the balcony above the dodgy bressummer beam and eventually came cascading down. The roof above the utility room on the first-floor landing was also suffering from waterlogging and one morning we found our bikes covered in damp white plaster after that ceiling had collapsed, too.

We stored our bikes in the empty ground-floor flat instead. Five days after Nell was born, with Nicola and the baby asleep upstairs, thieves broke in through the garage at the rear of the house. They went through the overgrown garden and smashed a back window in the empty flat on the ground floor, nicked our bikes and carried them out of the sash window at the front. If they were crack addicts, they had certainly come to the right house.

Now we didn't even feel safe in our home. Little Nell was a week old and her Dickensian name was beginning to seem increasingly appropriate. My patience had ended. In the most traumatic moments of my life I have always favoured the Wilkins J. Micawber approach of responding to adversity – that of writing lengthy letters and massive missives.

The insurance company were bellying the verticality levels of our lives. Highbury Barn now had three delis, while we had one flat that looked as if it was in an earthquake zone. The insurers had delayed too long and now they were going to get sarcasm and literary references and a little bit of pomposity. Nicola had tried being pleasant to them for six years. Now they were going to be hit with a metaphorical bressummer beam.

My letter was addressed to the chief executive. It pointed out that, after a six-year struggle, during which time his company had elevated procrastination to an art form, we were no closer to repairing the subsidence problems in our building. Consequently, we had a flat in a prime area of Highbury worth nearly a quarter of a million pounds which we were unable to sell.

It detailed how subsidence problems were first noted in 1995. How we now had huge foam-filled cracks in the exterior walls, the windows were crooked, a ceiling had collapsed and two tenants in the lower flats had left because of the appalling state of the house, and how we had been burgled as a direct result of the ground-floor flat being vacant.

Since 1995, there had been an endless round of reports, monitoring and visits from men in suits, with the work twice being put out to tender but never started. The property was deteriorating all the time and any work would now be all the more expensive.

Furthermore, the insurers were now arguing that no rebuilding of walls was necessary, and were instead advocating 'strapping'. It seemed extraordinary, after nearly seven years of meetings, by which time the insurers' professional, highly qualified staff could probably have completed a sequel to Proust's *Remembrance of Things Past* and must surely have known every brick, crack, crevice and collapsed portion of waterlogged plaster in the property in intimate detail, that their representatives were now contemplating a complete change of approach.

My letter added that if the insurers were so confident of the durability of Nicola's flat, we were quite happy to sell it to them for the market value, before noting that the company's mission statement contained some nonsense about delivering for customers. I ranted: 'By the time you deliver at Aubert Park these customers fully expect Godot to have arrived and the Christian world to be rejoicing at the Second Coming.' Not that I was becoming a man obsessed, oh no.

In conclusion, my letter demanded categorical assurance that 'you will take action this day to remedy the situation and begin rebuilding work and provide written assurances that we will be re-housed in suitable local accommodation at the earliest opportunity'.

Then, in the hope that the threat of some bad press might force the insurers to do something beyond filling our cracks with foam, I added that we were both journalists.

Copies of my epic letter were dispatched to *Which?* and the *Daily Mirror*'s Sorted column, neither of which thought the case worthy of pursuit – no doubt tardy insurers not doing subsidence work was so common it was unnecessary to comment further. Once I had campaigned for a Labour government, democratic socialism and an end to homelessness; now I was fighting for underpinning works.

Two weeks later we received an apologetic letter from the managing director's 'troubleshooter', presumably a sort of James Bond of verticality levels who liked his walls shaken not stirred. He did at least apologise and wrote that he hoped to 'rebuild our confidence' in his company. Rebuilding our house would have been better, though.

He added that it was their intention 'to make the property acceptable to potential purchasers'. Now he was going to take action. After six years of meetings, the insurers were going to categorically do something and, erm, hold an emergency meeting at our flat.

In late March, seven men in suits arrived at our crumbling flat, looking like a Home Counties version of the heist team from *Reservoir Dogs*. Here they were, beards newly trimmed, driving in from Surrey and Hertfordshire to pull off a job; troubleshooter Mr Bond, Mr Brick, Mr Wall, Mr Crack, Mr Foam, Mr Verticality and Nice Guy Eddie. They met the freeholder and drank real coffee and went outside to look at the bellying of the flank wall once again. Mr Bond announced that they were installing a new loss adjuster.

The new engineer was present, although rather worryingly he was going through a divorce and sleeping in his car, and announced that of course the strapping would work. The loss adjuster added that 'there was more than one way to skin a cat'. We decided to go with their strapping option, even if it did seem a bit too much like Meccano. Another man in a suit produced a bar graph that he'd knocked up on his computer as a provisional schedule of building works. This was a 'timeframe'. It seemed to suggest that the work would start within a few months and be finished within a year. Then again, it might just have been a picture of his graphic equaliser.

It seemed my literary abuse had had some effect. Godot was in a taxi outside and the engine was running with an impatient minicab driver inside. We were told that we could start looking for rented accommodation and move out as soon as we found somewhere comparable, and that the loss adjuster would pay for the rent while the subsidence work was being carried out.

Not only was I a rent boy again, I'd reduced Nicola to it as well. But at least our new home would be free; although Nicola would have to carry on paying the mortgage on her flat while the subsidence work continued. Since the property ladder was still submerged somewhere in a crevice beneath our bellying flank wall, this was indeed a result (we couldn't have afforded the market rents in Highbury at the time) – even if we did have to wait six and a half years for it.

We looked at seven two-bedroom places in one week. Rents in Islington were as preposterous as the house prices. At least there were plenty of properties available, though, as half the country seemed to have bought extra homes as buy-to-lets. Everything we tried for through estate agents was between £350 and £425 a week. Unless you were a barrister or a future Prime Minister, you just couldn't live in Islington anymore. One place we viewed, a dark basement flat off Upper Street with rotting windows, was on offer for £425 a week.

Only then we saw a two-bedroom house going in Whistler Street, a delightful, secluded street just off Drayton Park and a short walk from Highbury Fields. It was 'only' £300 a week, or £1,300 pcm. Although this sum could probably have saved countless kids' lives in the developing world, in Islington it was a knock-down deal. The house had a small L-shaped garden too, so Nicola would at last be able to grow her cherished runner beans. We accepted within the hour and the loss adjuster was happy to agree to it.

We were out of our crack den and renting again. Que sera, sera. Whatever will be will be. We're staying in Highbury. Forever.

MORTGAGE PROSPECTS: The applicant is now in an advantageous position to expedite his climb onto the property ladder, at least on paper. His household has two incomes – albeit below average – and his partner is a posh bird who has a bit put by in her trust fund and a flat to sell in a desirable location, close to Tubes, railway and all amenities. However, on his freelance earnings, the applicant is not eligible for a mortgage big enough to buy even a utility room. We recommend that the applicant waits for the subsidence in his partner's flat to be cured and makes sure that he doesn't leave the tap dripping, the loo seat up or upset her in any way if he wishes to break into the housing market.

AVERAGE HOUSE PRICE IN GREATER LONDON: £188,342

13. Verticality Crisis

Whistler Street, Highbury, London N5
April 2001 to January 2004

My life was in boxes. For the first time in three decades of London living, my stuff was being moved by a professional removal company rather than a Thatcherite bloke in a white van or a mate in a battered estate that could never quite fit in the top of my desk. Once, my bags would have been lugged across London on the Tube. Twenty years later, the operation had evolved into a proper removal van with three blokes moving us over two days. And the insurance company was paying for everything.

The removal men were even packing for us. This was a huge help, as with an eight-week-old baby and a two-year-old daughter, we were fully occupied. Into the van went the subsidence-surviving furniture, Nicola's numerous ornaments from around the globe, endless cardboard boxes, Lola's huge wicker basket full of toys and mountains of children's books. The removal men had even managed to box some of the finds made in Nicola's office area, a process that was marginally more time-consuming than the excavation of the Valley of the Kings.

Three crates of our things were put into storage. It wasn't that we had a lot of stuff or were hoarders, you understand, but we did seem to be both moving several cities' worth of possessions and storing enough items to keep a lunar colony going for 365 days. The itemised list read: one wardrobe, one desk (in three parts), one chair, one basket, one pine table (small), one chair (loose, marked all over), one desk (loose, marked all over), one cabinet, one trunk, two suitcases, fifteen pictures, one cassette box, one small flat-pack table, one small cabinet, one CD box, one flat-pack shelf, one small bin, one cooker, one fridge freezer, one chest of drawers (one leg broken), one chest of drawers (no leg broken), three rugs, two mats, one mirror, one heater and six garden tools.

Rather worryingly, the storage company had a list of possible defects for the stored goods which covered bent, broken, burned, chipped, contents and conditions unknown, dented, faced, gouged, loose, marked, mildewed, moth-eaten, rubbed, rusted, scratched, short, soiled, torn, badly worn and cracked. Our excess belongings seemed to come under just about every one of these categories in some form or another. Still, we believed in the principle of re-use, recycle and we were not throwing anything away, ever.

Even more thorough than the storage list was the inventory for the new house. A woman from the estate agents came round and ticked off every piece of assorted junk in the attic, every picture, every lamp, chair, light bulb, knife and fork, fish slice and scuff on the radiators. The National Census could probably have been completed in less time. Once that was over, we were in.

Whistler Street was two minutes away from Aubert Park. It was an old cobbled street covered in a veneer of splitting tarmac, full of former railway workers' cottages built in the late-nineteenth century. It had a distinctly northern feel to it. The front doors faced directly onto the narrow street. Everything was two-up, two-down with a small garden latched onto the back of the house. In fact, it was so northern-looking that it had been used as Liverpool in Terence Davies' 1988 film *Distant Voices, Still Lives*.

Whistler Street was U-shaped and had two entrances onto Drayton Park. There was barely room for residents to park their cars and if any vehicles met on the street, one would have to do some hasty reversing. It must have been the only place in London where kids still safely played football in the street.

Our new house had a friendly feel to it: it was light and, as the estate agents would put it, well appointed. The landlord was a skilled joiner who lived in Sweden and the place was covered in fine woodwork: a carved mantelpiece above the fireplace, cupboards with folding doors, and shelves and wooden radiator covers were everywhere. And, for once, we almost had enough storage space.

Although the houses in Whistler Street were basically cottages, in our property the corridor and partitions had been removed and the ground floor was one open-plan room. The kitchen had an expensive black-granite worktop, fitted cupboards and oak flooring. There was a gas hob above an electric fan oven. The windows fitted. There didn't seem to be a crack anywhere. Everything was finished. It was a grown-up house. As it should have been for £300 a week.

We had office space, too. The attic had been converted and a tiny set of wooden steps led up to a space that was big enough to fit in both of our computers and desks. There was still some storage space up there which was just too tempting for Nicola; she immediately used the spare loft space to deposit her boxes of environmental law tomes and 300 books all saying that climate change is a bad thing. They stayed there, unopened, for the duration of our stay. But they did make for very good insulation and we were seldom cold.

Once you were up in the attic, there was a trap door to keep the kids out. I could be enclosed in my own writer's den. The view through the small skylight revealed London as a real city, not just a collection of disconnected streets. The panorama stretched across the railway lines at Drayton Park and over to the trees and spires of Highgate, Muswell Hill and Alexandra Palace.

The only slight disadvantage to the house was that it had more spotlights than the Hammersmith Odeon. The owner was clearly a fastidious man who had taken huge pride in doing up his house. But did he love lights. Spotlights were set in the bathroom and kitchen ceilings, there was a huge rack of them in the living room and there was also a contrivance in the shape of a breast. This required standing on a stepladder undoing something called a 'nipple' before you could get at the bulb.

I'd lived in flats with bare bulbs before but this place had the inverse problem. Everything was just too stylish and sophisticated. There was a set of lights on the landing that required miniature, one-centimetre-long bulbs. Some lights needed screw-in bulbs, others needed the clip-in variety. For some, I had to take complex fittings apart and for others, I was required to master several spring-loaded clips. None were simple, standard bulbs and they were all impossible to replace. I'd find myself trawling John Lewis, Waitrose, the hardware shops at Highbury Barn and Finsbury Park, or Homebase on Seven Sisters Road in increasingly futile attempts to find French-made Sylvania bulbs that had a straight not tapered screw-in fitting.

Islington style was all very well, but unless you owned a lighting shop it was impossible to maintain. Nor could you fit energy-saving bulbs in the endless racks of lights that should have been in Will and Grace's apartment and not in our family home. When the transformer in the living room went and a whole rack of poncy ceiling spotlights were disabled, we just gave up and used the remaining relatively simple screw-in bulb fittings and our own lamp. How many tenants does it take to change a light bulb? None, because you can't get hold of the bulbs.

Apart from the bulbs, though, high-class renting had several advantages. If any repairs were needed, we simply phoned the estate agent which then sent a man round. When the washing machine broke down it was replaced in days.

From Whistler Street, an enticing alleyway led up Framfield Road to Highbury Fields. We made many a trip with Lola on her wooden pedal-free Like-a-Bike and Nell in the buggy to the Fields, the Oasis Café and the playground by Highbury Pool. Squirrels and Clive Anderson roamed among the daffodils and trees. Highbury and Islington Tube was now only a brisk ten-minute walk away.

The alleyway up towards the Fields also served as an unofficial dumping ground for all sorts of bulky refuse. A few weeks into our stay, I met Nicola and her mother carrying an ancient, white cushion-less sofa towards the house. 'This is worth £600!' she kept saying, even though we already had one working sofa. Nicola's mum, Fiona, believed in make do and mend. So did Nicola, except she called it recycling. Our house was already starting to resemble Alfred and Harold Steptoe's gaff. For a green hoarder like Nicola –

and now my daughters too, who loved picking up street detritus – that alleyway was to be a perennial source of clutter/treasure.

Whistler Street was a bizarre mix of middle-class and local-authority tenants. The middle classes had barbecues and house-warming parties and joined the Whistler Street Association, while a small minority of the local-authority residents seemed to have been sent by Mike Leigh to audition for the role of noisy neighbours. Because the street was so narrow, our neighbours were only ten feet across the road and as summer approached we soon discovered that we could hear every word of every effing argument.

We had several 'characters' in the vicinity. There was Mad Jane who apparently had a very sad personal story and would shout and holler things in the night. There was a drunken Mancunian bloke who would sometimes return home even more inebriated than usual and go to the wrong house. At 1 a.m., we'd hear cries of 'No, go home, you haven't lived in this house for 11 years!' At other times, he'd collapse in the road with his faithful dog sitting by his prone form waiting for him to regain consciousness.

Another local character would wander up and down the street all day smoking and drinking cans of lager while talking to himself about Rodney King and racism. One Sunday morning, we were woken by the sound of Mad Jane's door being kicked in by an irate neighbour, drunk and full of aggression because she'd woken his gran up with her nocturnal shouting. Thankfully, the police (who must have been virtual season-ticket holders at the houses of some of the miscreants) were called, which was a big relief because Nicola was just about to send me out to deal with Mr Psycho in my dressing gown.

Periodically, the old offices at the bottom of the street would attract Spanish squatters with dreadlocks who would merge with the regular posse of misfits. It would have been a perfect hangout for Dustin Hoffman in his *Midnight Cowboy* phase.

But, in the main, Whistler Street was a peaceful place with a real sense of community. Those neighbours who were not kicking each other's doors in did actually talk to each other. Nicola's brother moved in a few doors down the street from us and when he was burgled it was two of the street-football kids who phoned the police after they saw a druggie with a bin bag climbing out of his window. The police were astonished that any street in London still had such neighbourliness. We'd be scrubbing our doorsteps and having a knees-up round the old Joanna soon.

But the odd street row or party in the summer sounded all the more cacophonous because neither of us were getting any sleep. Since the move, baby Nell had developed eczema, something now suffered by an astonishing one in five infants, compared to one in thirty half a century ago. She had to sleep in a gloved suit and was routinely held down by one of us on each arm throughout the night. Life was an itch. Routinely, we'd be woken up on the hour to try and stop another scratch attack.

Nell's skin would become red, dry and itchy, then blister and weep. If we left her alone or ungloved, she scratched until she drew blood – hence Operation Pindown. If we turned away for a second, those super-sharp kiddie talons, however short they might be cut, would cause wounds that made her look like she'd just encountered Edward Scissorhands. Often the wounds would became infected, requiring steroid creams or oral antibiotics and leaving us agonising about her long-term health.

As we tried all the recommended solutions, we realised the limitations of renting with a young family. The fact that a cat had lived there before us aggravated her skin. We tried turning off the heating and opening windows and cutting out dairy products. Doctors said dust mites were a major problem, so we fitted dust-mite covers to the bedding but what we really needed to do was take up the carpets. The landlord didn't want us to do this – even in the bathroom where we had offered to pay for a new wooden floor – so we were stuck with them. Still, once the subsidence was cured, I reassured Nicola, we could sell her place and buy a house with stripped wooden floors, just like everyone else in Highbury.

Only the subsidence work on her flat was some way from being completed. Or even started. For five months, Nicola's flat, and indeed the entire building, stood empty. It was astonishing. Having procrastinated for six years, the insurance company was now paying £300 a week for us to rent in Whistler Street and compensating the freeholder for the loss of rent in the two flats below. Yet this wasted expense did not seem to worry them. Still, no doubt they were having plenty of meetings about the property and writing lots of departmental e-mails marked 'Action This Millennium'.

We were a little worried about squatters moving in, but even they seemed to spot the wonky windows and cracks of doom, and move on to somewhere more solid. The thought occurred to me that if we'd known it would be empty for five months, we could have rented it to some short-life licensees – once we had fitted some asbestos inside the walls, that is.

Finally, as autumn arrived, the tender for the work was assigned to a company in Essex and the workmen moved in. The empty house was covered in scaffolding. The initial work seemed bizarrely low tech: just two men with a wheelbarrow who were digging out clay and soil from around the cellar foundations.

As the work started, we watched the television coverage of the 11 September terrorist attacks on New York and wondered if it was safe to stay in London. I went up to my office in the attic and looked out at the lights in the night sky, wondering which planes were destined to drop on London. Nicola was convinced that the world economic system would collapse anyway and that this was the end of everything. And, not that we were self-interested at all, that one of the first companies to go under would be our insurers – with no house to sell, we might as well flee to North Wales. But the world did eventually return to some kind of normality. The war was fought in Afghanistan and the work on the house in Aubert Park continued.

Earlier that year, my aunt Audrey in Stoke died at the age of 80. She had left everything to my two sisters and me. As an executor of the will, one of my tasks was to sell her house so that the proceeds could be divided between us.

Whenever I could, I travelled up to Stoke to clear out the house and have it valued. It soon became clear that Britain was a country of two property-owning nations, the North and South.

Audrey and her late husband Arthur had lived in a three-bedroom house in Dresden, a relatively middle-class part of the Potteries. Arthur had been an architect for the local authority. He designed and built their home, which they had bought soon after the Second World War ended.

In many ways, my aunt and uncle epitomised the post-war property dream. Both from relatively working-class backgrounds, they had aspired to middle-class home ownership.

My uncle had fought in Burma in the war and would often tell tales of walking for three days without any food before finding British forces who offered him a slice of bread and jam – the best meal he'd ever had. Or he would say that if you had seen some of the things he'd seen, such as dogs eating human heads, then you would be grateful to live in a peaceful England.

Exemplary examples of that pride in home ownership which is peculiar to Britain, they seemed content in their new home, listening to Frank Sinatra records and marvelling at the features my uncle had installed when he designed the house: things such as central heating, built-in wardrobes and a teasmaid.

Yet Audrey's home was valued at just £52,000. In London, it would have been worth £300,000 more than that. The pottery and mining industries had gone and unemployment in the region was high. One survey carried out at the time had listed Stoke-on-Trent as the least desirable place to live in Britain, which seemed a little unfair: the houses were cheap and during my visits everyone was unfailingly friendly.

My dad, still anticipating the next property slump, suggested that I should buy out my sisters and move into my aunt's cheap home. But, although buying in a cheaper market was logical, it was hard to persuade ourselves of the merits of post-industrial Stoke with its blackened buildings and high unemployment. Both of our jobs and most of our friends also still lay in London.

My days as a property magnate were restricted by Nell's eczema. The sleepless nights were putting my relationship with Nicola under a huge strain and it was never possible to spend more than one night at a time in Stoke. While Nell was still shackled in gloved suits that looked like they belonged in Guantanamo Bay, I was also immersing myself in the 2001–02 football season, working on my book *West Ham: Irons in the Soul*. Time and energy were limited for this knackered dad.

Given a few weeks in the Potteries, it might have been possible to emulate all those nauseatingly cheerful TV presenters with tools on their belts in the plethora of property programmes sweeping British TV. The walls were stained with 50-odd years' worth of nicotine as both my aunt and uncle were heavy smokers. Ideally, these should have been painted white to attract new buyers and a fitted kitchen and new bathroom installed to up the price ten grand or so. The windows were rotting in places too, but it was still a potentially fine home. As it was, all I could do was cut the grass, clear the place and put it on the market as it stood.

Eventually, it fetched £51,500. It seemed ironic and extremely sad that the home my aunt and uncle had built and invested so much hope in should be selling for the price of half a bedroom in London.

Progress ground on slowly at the Aubert Park flat during 2002. The contractor's main policy seemed to be to fill the place with holes. We still had keys and when we went in it looked like Jack Nicholson had been attacking every wall with an axe. Every partition wall had holes through it. There was damp coming through the bedroom ceiling and numerous floorboards were up. Scaffolding came through the brickwork as if it were the only structure holding the whole edifice together. Half the banisters were missing. A green tarpaulin covered the sodden bressummer beam in the ground-floor flat. The garden was full of distressed furniture, planks, rubble and builder's detritus. Still, at least all the destruction had persuaded the mice to scarper.

We wondered if we might end up living in rubber tyres. Whenever there was a ridiculously inflated property market, people always suggested new forms of affordable housing. Back in the 1980s, there had been that idea of 'mingle units' and earlier in 2002 flat-pack homes described as 'micro-units' were being advertised. In July, the latest idea was 'earthships' – affordable houses made from Britain's 40 million discarded tyres. The tyres would be filled with earth and then used to create a dwelling in which you'd never be tyred of life, at a cost of £40,000. Presumably, some innovative owner of a house on Skid Row would call his new home Mull of Kin Tyres.

Maybe other discarded everyday objects would also soon be used to build low-cost housing. Britain's mountain of discarded fridges might be transformed into huge white bricks that fitted together, providing cheap accommodation for those frozen out of the housing market. Nicola said people in PNG lived in transport containers and you could see it happening here too.

It was going to take more than a few tyres to sort out our housing situation in Highbury. Eventually, the brickwork on the front wall started to be rebuilt and at least the windows looked straight. But by mid-2002, there were huge problems with piles. This was nothing to do with the engineer's posterior but something to do with the concrete which was going to form the base of the strapping. Indeed, there was so much talk of strapping that it almost seemed the flat was part of the growing fetish shopping scene in Holloway Road, at places like Fettered Pleasures.

Finally, the piles were cured and the frame was in place. In the hope that Jarndyce and Jarndyce Construction Ltd might eventually finish work on the Aubert Park property, we started testing the still hyper-inflated London property market. Houses on our street, basically two-bedroom cottages, were going for £350,000 to £400,000. What was most striking for us was not just the prices, but the attempt to sell a lifestyle. We were shown around one house in which every book, magazine and ornament had been cunningly chosen. All that was missing was the smell of baking bread. There was the Ingrid Bergman biography by the bed, a guide to walks in Paris downstairs, endless copies of *National Geographic*, a couple of travel books, an ethnic African sculpture in the fireplace, a bottle of chardonnay in the fitted kitchen and even framed pictures of a family on the living-room desk. Which was all very atmospheric until the estate agent revealed that the house was previously rented and had been empty for weeks. The possessions inside were simply props to sell a lifestyle – stylish but inoffensive – to impressionable buyers. I did wonder if we should do the same with Nicola's flat, should it ever be ready for sale. No doubt a discreetly placed packet of Huggies, a pile of West Ham programmes and an empty six-pack of lager would create just the ambience we needed to bag that sale.

By the end of the year, Nicola was being asked for paint scheme and carpet recommendations. Soon we would be able to sell the flat and invest in our own property. Still, even with the revenue from that sale, we might struggle to pay the massive prices in London. We surveyed other areas such as Oxford and Bath, almost succumbing to the middle-class dream of moving to the country.

Nicola worked hard installing a new bathroom and some wooden flooring in her flat in the anticipation that she could sell it quickly and we could carry on renting in Whistler Street until we bought somewhere else. We had the place valued by an estate agent who said that a new kitchen and bathroom would put £20,000 on the selling price. Nicola didn't want to play the greed game, but knew that unless we got the maximum price for her flat we'd never be able to buy anywhere else in London. Everyone is trapped in the cycle of ever-higher house prices.

The bathroom was installed by a local firm without any problem. Nicola ordered a new fitted kitchen from a leading DIY store in New Southgate in September 2002. This was the final lifestyle statement that would surely entice affluent City people or barristers to buy the flat.

The verticality crisis was over, allegedly, but the capacity for property to sabotage my life still appeared infinite. All my hopes, dreams and aspirations of placing one tiny toe on the greasy rungs of the property ladder were now to be wrecked by a sodding kitchen.

From January, we were paying the £300 rent at Whistler Street ourselves. It was expensive, but it would only be for a few months until the flat was sold and we had purchased a home. The only problem was the kitchen. The company had insisted on the £1,500 payment before they started work. Three months after Nicola first stepped into the store at New Southgate, the kitchen hadn't arrived. The old kitchen had been taken out by the builders and only a series of pipes sticking out of the wall remained where there should have been an environment fit for Jamie Oliver.

After numerous letters and calls, we discovered that the man who had taken three hours to draw up the plans had been working on his first-ever kitchen and unfortunately seemed to have no concept of measurement. No wonder he'd confided to Nicola that he really wanted to be a scriptwriter. He'd taken a wok on the wild side and the whole thing was completely wrong. New plans had to be made and the kitchen re-ordered. Nicola put her flat on the market regardless. She placed a hopeful framed picture of the Verona Cherry kitchen in the empty room to give an impression of how it would eventually look. Sadly, all of the prospective buyers seemed to want the real thing.

The estate agent confidently predicted it would fetch at least £240,000, but without the kitchen in place no one even made an offer. A generation brought up on *Location, Location, Location* wanted flats that were ready to move into straight away. Our promise that the kitchen would be fitted by the time they moved in meant nothing. I thought I had experienced every difficulty there was connected to property, but no, there was always something unexpected waiting to get you. Now nemesis was coming via a Verona Cherry kitchen.

Oh, and there was a war breaking out. US troops were massing around Iraq and it was clear that President Bush would soon be heading into conflict regardless of what the weapons inspectors hadn't found. Tony Blair was sending British troops in too, despite huge protest marches against the war. Every house in Islington seemed to have a 'Not In My Name' poster in its window. Having talked up prices, the estate agents were now saying that the market was very slow, because no one wanted to make a decision about buying property in the build-up to a war that could last for weeks or years.

An attack on a Muslim country could provoke terrorist strikes against London; oil prices might soar if the conflict was a long one and the world might move into recession. And with all those weapons of mass destruction that Tony Blair said Saddam Hussein possessed – and he was a pretty straight sort of guy – who knew what evil might be unleashed?

As the troops went on the offensive, so did we over the kitchen. In the time it took to assemble a third of the British armed forces in the Gulf, our DIY firm hadn't yet managed to master the logistics of sending a kitchen from New Southgate to Highbury.

The problem was that it was a new store with new staff and none of them seemed to know anything about kitchens. The company troubleshooter was very apologetic and said that most of the staff who had taken our botched order had now moved on. She was having to stand in the warehouse picking out the kitchen herself, she said, and there were around 50 other equally dissatisfied customers. Whenever we spoke to her or the manager, the kitchen was always two days away.

We tried writing direct to the managing director and were then put onto his personal troubleshooter. It was starting to resemble the subsidence saga with the insurance company. You wondered how M15 ever recruited anyone when there were so many troubleshooters working in private industry. At one point, someone at the warehouse told me, in true Basil Fawltyesque fashion, 'Don't talk to anyone on the floor, you might as well try talking to a monkey.'

One option might have been to move back into Nicola's flat to try and save money, but without a kitchen we couldn't. We had a flat that we couldn't sell, rent out or move back into and were losing money as a direct consequence of inept kitchen sellers. It was exasperating.

In February 2003, we discovered that the entire warehouse had been evacuated. There had been a fire next door and apparently our order had been 'dissolved' by smoke. So we had to fax it again, only the fax machine wasn't working for the following two days.

The staff always seemed very pleased with themselves when they did manage to get a part for our kitchen, as if one part out of fifty-seven was somehow a huge achievement. Mind you, at that store it was. We were still being assured that the cupboard doors were arriving in two days while the manager claimed that a hob was on the way from North Finchley.

The store's troubleshooter then took several weeks off through illness (which was surely understandable given the organisation she worked for). I began to write about the kitchen saga in my column in *Midweek*, read by 130,000 Londoners, but even bad publicity didn't seem to worry them. The ruder I became, the tardier their service.

Meanwhile, property prices in London had gone down for two months running. Was this the '80s all over again? It girl Tara Palmer-Tomkinson had declared that 'Renting is the new black', saying of her west London flat: 'I am not tied to one property and I do not shudder every time interest rates are mentioned . . . all the maintenance is the landlord's responsibility.'

Just as *Relocation, Relocation* attracted 5.3 million viewers on Channel 4, the market appeared to be falling. What would the presenters of the likes of *Location, Location, Location* and *Escape to the Sun* do now? Be re-employed on *Repossession, Repossession, Repossession* telling families like ourselves how to turn council rooms into icons of style or make a period feature of one-bar electric fires and 1970s wallpaper?

At the start of March, we did receive some breakfast bars (which was a poncy name for worktops). Only then a troubleshooter (all these troubleshooters could have formed their own expeditionary force to Iraq) phoned us on a Saturday night, sounding like he'd had a few stress-relieving beers, with some bad news. They had discovered that the breakfast bars would be too wide and that we actually needed Mayan worktops. Fine.

Other bits of kitchen arrived in small consignments. We were getting to know John the company driver quite well, particularly his dodgy clutch cable, which always seemed to go when there was an Arsenal game live on Sky. The revolutionary idea of delivering all the parts that constitute a fitted kitchen in one consignment had not as yet penetrated the psyches of the line managers and troubleshooters.

We were beginning to understand how Odysseus felt on his ten-year voyage home from the Trojan wars, always being reassured that Ithaca was only two islands away.

Finally, at the end of March, some seven months after first ordering the bloody thing, the final box arrived. At the DIY store,

VERTICALITY CRISIS

J.D. Salinger would have been considered a prodigious and speedy wordsmith. After waiting for 196 days (that's some 282,240 minutes), the shock of the final delivery was acute. All I could do was sit gibbering in the corner, clutching the two Mayan worktops and refusing to let anyone touch them lest our dream of a new kitchen was snatched away again.

But hope was worse than despair. The kitchen fitter arrived and announced that we were missing three wall end panels, three base end panels, one corner blanking panel, and we had the wrong size Mayan worktops. No wonder the Mayan civilisation collapsed. I had no idea what a blanking panel was, but could picture myself smashing them over several people's heads.

That kitchen company had achieved what terrorist threats from Osama bin Laden, war and destruction in Iraq, even West Ham's defending that season by Minto, Breen, Dailly and Repka had failed to do. My spirit was shattered. God was dead. World peace would never be achieved. There was no kitchen and there never would be one. Nicola's savings and my aunt's inheritance were disappearing rapidly. The last vestiges of sanity were slipping away. It would have been tempting to do a Sylvia Plath if only the gas oven and hob had been fitted.

It seemed there was no possibility of blanking panel closure in our kitchen-sink drama. But against all expectations one or two pieces of hardware did start to filter through the myopic ordering departments and ended up at our house. A couple of worktops arrived and then some base end panels. Finally, late one Saturday night, the blanking panels appeared. I still have no idea what they do, beyond possibly encasing the dilithium crystals on the USS *Enterprise*, but at least they were blanking well here.

There was still the kitchen fitter to book, of course, and no doubt he would hold us up for a fortnight before arriving in his white van and announcing that the blanking panel verticality ioniser was malfunctioning.

But no, 26 April 2003 saw one giant leap in the history of Verona Cherry kitchens. It was installed. We opened a bottle of champagne and slumped onto a base end panel, finally saved from blanking panel property oblivion. The kitchen had only taken seven and a half months to arrive. It was not made of gold but it did look quite good. Brave Odysseus had finally returned to Ithaca. Penelope, we're back, and tell your suitors we're going to hit them over the head with some blanking panels and then roast them on a spanking new gas hob.

So at last we had a kitchen. But now there was the problem of trying to sell the flat. Nicola placed it on the market with two estate agents for both sale and rent, so desperate were we to shift it. Paying a huge rent and the mortgage on the flat was just not feasible on our freelance and part-time incomes. We decided to give it two months, after which we would move back up the three flights of stairs to the two-bedroom, gardenless flat.

Nicola was still taking it all remarkably well, apart from the odd holler that her life had not moved on ever and nobody else had ever been so tormented over the kitchen and the subsidence and now she was going to end up back in the same flat that she had bought in 1989 and she wanted to plant trees and live in the same home for the rest of her life and why had she not met a merchant banker who knew how to put up shelves?

Bizarrely, having been told all my life to get on the property ladder, it now seemed that absolutely no one wanted to climb up to the third floor at Aubert Park. Despite the Verona Cherry kitchen. Nicola dropped the asking price by £20,000 but still no one even made an offer. It was never like this on the TV. It had only just been announced that the war in Iraq was finished and perhaps the flat's history of subsidence was putting people off. Although, like most Highbury residents, Nicola had learned through painful experience that it was much better to buy a place with the subsidence work already done, rather than wait for the property to collapse.

In June, we were saved. Two blokes who were friends of one of Nicola's colleagues at Friends of the Earth moved in to rent the place. At last, we had some income against our outgoings. We were still down on the Whistler Street rent but at least we could survive. Twenty-two years after moving to London, I was almost a landlord. Nicola was managing the property and in the first month we were busy moving chairs and dodgy wardrobes over to the grateful tenants. I thought of Mr Draper at Comeragh Road and wondered if soon I'd be withholding their deposit for not washing the curtains. Although greed and property are intertwined in Britain, we resolved to be benevolent landlords, if that's not an oxymoron. Just as long as they didn't complain about that dodgy wardrobe we found in someone's garden.

The flat was let but we wondered what we should do next. My aunt's estate had finally been settled and she had left me around £70,000. This would help with a deposit for a house and I was very lucky to be benefiting from inherited wealth. But as the average price for a house in London in 2003 was £236,470, it still wasn't enough. The Iraq war scare had only been a three month blip in the market and prices were moving remorselessly upwards again. Nicola could raid what was left in her trust fund, but without selling her flat we would still need a hefty mortgage. Once again, the problems of a decreasing freelance income, a part-time job and large childcare bills conspired to make home ownership almost unattainable.

It could have been worse. Whistler Street was overcrowded, but still a great, if expensive, place to live. Lola was by this stage in the reception class at the local school. A compensation dispute over the kitchen rumbled on but, in the end, after we threatened to go to the small claims court for our four months' lost rent, the company gave us the kitchen for free. So at least we had gained something from the sorry saga and Nicola's tenants were benefiting from a kitchen that had been lovingly marinated for over seven long months in a warehouse in New Southgate.

We let any housing decision wait until after the six weeks of school summer holidays. While house-sitting in Yorkshire, Nicola spotted a castle for sale for a mere £330,000, less than the price of a two-bedroom cottage in Whistler Street. She ordered the details and was posh enough to be taken seriously by the vendors, who no doubt thought that I was her faithful retainer and odd-job man. Although in half of the castle the rooms were furnished, the other half consisted of ruins, suffering from the sort of subsidence that even the men in suits monitoring our wall studs might have accepted was genuine. We decided that the running costs of a castle might be a little prohibitive and returned to London.

In the September sunshine, Highbury felt a little like Bedford Falls in *It's A Wonderful Life*. Doing a circuit of school and nursery and Highbury Fields, about five people stopped to talk to me, the man in the corner shop was friendly and we seemed to know everyone through the nursery, school and the ecology centre and the countless other committees Nicola had signed up for. It wasn't always like that, but there was a sense of community in Highbury that we both enjoyed. And you could meet people without owning a car, unlike in the country. Never mind the fact that Tunbridge Wells was just 42 minutes from Charing Cross and most of Highbury now wanted to move there. We liked it where we were.

It was time for what folks in marketing would refer to as some 'thinking outside the box'. If we couldn't sell the flat (the tenants were on a six-month renewable lease) then we would try to buy anyway. A visit to John Charcol Financial Advisers was most helpful. They suggested that, as we had a relatively high deposit to put down, we could obtain a self-certification mortgage. (It was indeed a great surprise that I hadn't as yet been self-certified after my 14 homes in London.)

Basically, self-certification meant that we could estimate our own incomes. I could count my turnover instead of my self-employment profit and Nicola could include the rental income from her flat (other mortgage companies had insisted that a property had to be let for three years before they would include it in your income). Some buyers have got into trouble through lying on self-certification mortgages, but for people like us who just wanted a little more flexibility, self-certification was perfect.

Lola liked her school and we were both on the PTA. Hell, we couldn't give up those positions of secretary and treasurer. If we were going to be indecisive, we might as well be indecisive in London. If we had an offer for a mortgage, we would buy here and worry about leaving London later. Maybe never.

During house viewings in early 2003, we had seen one two-storey property we liked in what the estate agents termed 'Arsenal Village' (not to be confused with Finsbury Park, oh no). It hadn't sold and the price had been reduced by £50,000. We looked at the place again. It was close to Finsbury Park mosque and the area had been cordoned off by police after a raid on alleged terrorist suspects. Outside broadcast vans were everywhere, with TV crews loitering in St Thomas's Road.

Maybe some buyers had been deterred by all the police activity, but it didn't worry us. We liked the fact that London is multicultural and knew that, when the media were not about, the area was a quiet place to live. Besides, as I may have mentioned before, a man who has survived one of Kirsty's notes, asbestos fibres, cockroaches, changed locks and a vase through the window can handle just about anything, including global terror networks.

The house had an eccentric charm; it was on the corner of two streets and had triangular-shaped rooms with a large back garden. Admittedly it also had Hilda Ogden carpets, pink wallpaper, lace curtains and bad-taste '70s fireplaces. But anyone who had seen any of the 3,000 property programmes currently airing on British TV would have known that these were superficial problems which could easily be remedied. It was close to the Tube and could always be rented if we moved out of London and there was room for a lodger should we become desperate for cash. We made an offer of £20,000 below the asking price – and it was ACCEPTED!

Could this be it? An end to my years as a rent boy? Admittedly, the vendor's solicitors in Hull did their best to keep me renting through some inept loss of deeds and forgetting to make their clients sign just about everything they needed to. There was always the fear of being gazumped and we knew that we could not hand in our notice at Whistler Street until exchange took place.

On 10 November 2003, I finally went to see Dexys again – 22 years after they'd inspired me through my rental sojourn across the capital. At the age of 44, I was once more experiencing that spiritual, uplifting feeling that follows a Dexys gig – the thrill of playing the songs I'd heard the night before on my CD player again, that pleasant ringing in the ears, the sense of having seen something special.

More knowing and self-deprecating than all those years ago, Kevin Rowland changed the lyrics of 'Tell Me When My Light Turns Green' to 'Seen quite a bit in my 49 years'. Kevin had been through a breakdown, 14 years of cocaine addiction, homelessness and wearing women's clothes. Only I'd endured something worse – the private rental sector. Never did I think that I'd come to experience the intense emotions Dexys had articulated so brilliantly many years ago not through wandering down Harrow Road in a state of heightened consciousness while trying to believe in my soul, as Kevin once did, but through trying to find somewhere to live.

We had both survived. I was about to buy a house, Kevin was drug-free, apologetic, finished with cross-dressing and feeling a surge of love from the audience at the Royal Festival Hall that must have inspired him. Welcome back, Kev, and if you're having any problems with building societies after those coke-addled years, then might I recommend a self-certification mortgage.

Nicola and I were very anxious to complete before Christmas, but three months after the offer was accepted the vendor's solicitors had forgotten to get him to sign the contract. Then they couldn't find the deeds. The mortgage offer came through (eventually) and our survey was satisfactory, but then there were concerns over the Thames Lee Tunnel which travelled beneath part of our garden. At first we thought it was some crumbling Victorian sewer, but a couple of calls to Thames Water revealed that it was only built in 1992 and was 60 feet underground, so we decided to let it flow.

There was still time for a final twist to the subsidence saga at Nicola's flat. The freeholder had tried to remortgage the ground floor flat, but had been refused a mortgage because cracks had appeared in the walls. Yes, the verticality crisis had returned. Cue the sound of our heads banging on tables. Oh, and a rat had been spotted in the basement, too.

It was lucky that we had already had the offer accepted on our new house, otherwise several insurance-company men might have been beaten around the head with useless pieces of steel strapping and blanking panels and then had studs inserted in their bellying flank walls for monitoring over seven years.

Several exasperated calls to the insurers ensured the return of the men with their studs. They deduced that there was a problem with the party wall; the three sides of the building they had worked on were fine, they claimed, it was just the rest of the street that was subsiding. We have discovered that insurance companies only solve current problems and never do pre-emptive work. They assured us that a week's building work in the summer of 2004 would end our verticality problems for good. Somehow we think it might not be that simple.

On 19 December, we still hadn't exchanged, with the lawyers' offices closing that day for the two-week festive holiday. Our solicitor was exasperated too. By this stage, I was imagining fax machines covered in cobwebs as blokes who looked like Tim from *The Office* prepared to go home to their Aged P. Only today, they were wearing paper hats and kicking conveyancing documents around the floor, as they sipped another paper cup of Christmas punch and fired off another streamer before dropping the deeds to my new house in the bin.

Just before five, the vendor's solicitors claimed that we owed £2,600 for fixtures and fittings, when it had been agreed that these were free. Thinking Basil Fawltyesque thoughts about thrashing legal types, I phoned the vendor, who agreed there was no charge. It turned out that his myopic solicitors had misread 'zero' on his fax as '£2,600'. We exchanged at 5 p.m., about 30 seconds before the legal fraternity scarpered for Christmas.

This was it. The property was legally ours, just as long as we came up with the deposit and some form of Armageddon didn't strike London within the next three or four weeks. My long day's journey through rental nightmares might finally be over.

MORTGAGE PROSPECTS: Much to our surprise, the applicant has finally been offered a self-certification mortgage. He and his partner have both benefited from inherited wealth and, after finally mastering the logistics of moving a kitchen across London, they may at last, barring the possibility of extraterrestrial invasions, terrorist strikes, the Thames Barrier collapsing, earthquakes, volcanic eruptions, plague or pestilence, be about to climb up the property ladder.

AVERAGE HOUSE PRICE IN GREATER LONDON: £236,470

14. PARK LIFE

Finsbury Park, London N4
January 2004 onwards

The house that I am sitting in is mine. Or at least most of it is mine. Excluding the bit that belongs to the mortgage company. That will be mine by the time I'm 65, just as long as I remain in work. But the bit that I paid the deposit on with my aunt's inheritance definitely belongs to me. It's tempting to become a brick hugger and embrace the very walls of the place.

Through the vagaries of my accommodation struggle, I have experienced and in many cases grown to love numerous areas of London. But now we have joined the majority of middle-class, cash poor–property rich Islingtonians struggling to pay the bills at Waitrose while sitting in houses that are apparently going up in value by the second.

We have a cellar for our collection of vintage 2002 wines. We can put picture hooks in the walls without asking the landlord. We can paint the walls any colour we want (and that pink in the hallway and kitchen certainly has to go). I can dig archaeological trenches in the garden with my daughters and no one can stop me. We can keep pets without anyone's permission. There are deeds on which my name is indelibly engraved.

After ten years of living in subsidence, Nicola and I had booked a provisional date for a wedding – only it fell on the day we planned the move and, rather than do the two most stressful things in your life at once, we decided to postpone our nuptials. Accommodation affects your life in so many ways. It was fitting really. Property has been the passion of my life; it was never going to be usurped by a mere woman.

Slowly, we are unpacking. We have two living rooms, one of which is currently stacked up to the ceiling with boxes. This will be our library once the man who has promised to build our shelves finally finds a diary window. So, for the moment, I just sit and admire my boxes.

Anyone who has ever moved house will recognise those mini-mountains of flat-packed cardboard. Simply place a cross of white masking tape on the bottom, pile in your books and CDs, seal up the top and you have the sturdiest of containers. In fact, they could provide a revolutionary new self-build material. They are solid but flexible; packing-box buildings would be ideal for earthquake zones.

Luckily they are reusable. It's much more interesting to study the previous user's instructions than unpack your things. You can tell someone's class simply from whether they use their marker pens to scrawl 'lounge' or 'drawing room' or 'study' on the top. Surely only someone desperately uncool and lower-middle class would label their box 'Habitat unit'. In a desperately upwardly mobile gesture, we have marked our own boxes for the second sitting room 'library'.

The study of boxes is compulsive (unfortunately it also means that I'm destined never to finish unpacking). One old box is marked 'Pussy cat – Sylvia'. Can you really move pets in boxes? And why has someone got a whole box marked 'Polish dictionaries'? Why do German stationery companies have such neatly printed instructions? Why do some individuals go to the trouble of printing out their own sticky labels rather than relying on felt pen? Why do some people use red tape and three strips of it on the bottom instead of two? Why is it that people are so honest in their box descriptions? No doubt there are boxes labelled 'sex aids' and 'blow-up doll' somewhere in our huge collection.

Of course, now that we've moved, we've forgotten what half the labels mean and in some cases the removal men followed the previous mover's instructions. There's the thrill of slitting open that tape with a serrated knife, never quite sure what's lying inside and then discovering your kitchen things in 'Bedroom One'.

It would have been a shame to leave possibly my last-ever rented house without a row over the deposit. The estate agent is trying to charge us £800-plus for various felonies. There's £100 because the French light bulbs in the bathroom that no one can find anywhere in England have not been replaced and it's £60 just to call a man out to replace them and, of course, estate agents can't possibly change light bulbs themselves, even if we pay for them.

Then there's the £250 for the broken shower tap in the bathroom, £20 for the stained shower curtain, £5 for the missing plastic bowl and £65 for some scuff marks on the walls. And, although we paid £300 to have the house industrially vacuumed when we left, they are still asking for a further £350 for cleaning. Nicola spent two days scrubbing the place when we left. Either she's a very bad cleaner or the spirit of Mr Draper at Comeragh Road lives on. As ever with landlord and tenant, there is some dispute about what constitutes fair wear and tear following a three-year stay. We have now reached a compromise settlement which still leaves us £600 down.

But at least we are now here in our home, having given several removal men hernias with our lorry full of clutter. We have been doing all those things you see on property programmes. The house was relatively cheap for Highbury Borders (oh, all right, Finsbury Park) because it was full of '70s decor. So now all our money is going on getting rid of it.

The lace curtains and the gas fire in the living room have gone and two blokes have removed the tiled abomination of a fireplace in our bedroom and exposed the old brickwork from 1870. The three carpets upstairs (yellow swirls, purple and grey) had to go and a man is coming to sand the floors at some indeterminate future date.

For the first two weeks here, we had to live without a cooker. Chris, the Greek plumber who's lived in Holloway Road for 50 years and whose sister runs the Olive Tree restaurant in Blackstock Road, insisted that the cooker the previous owner left us as part of the fixtures and fittings was 'a death trap'. He said it was leaking gas and had to be removed at once.

The loo was cracked and the cistern soon smashed and that had to be replaced too. The arch above the garden gate has been repointed. New Banham locks have been put on the front door and the louvre windows in the kitchen will soon be replaced by a double-glazed sash. Like those horrible people at dinner parties that I used to curse throughout the '80s and '90s, I can now hear some inner voice saying that, although we have spent thousands of pounds, we have already increased the value of our property by £20,000.

And, having discovered that tradesmen will soon be the new aristocracy (through the prices they charge freelance journalists), financial necessity has compelled me to learn how to operate a screwdriver. The world's most eminently unpractical man has just successfully repaired the garden gate.

The girls like their new home. On their first night here, their beds were up and their favourite stories on hand. We go Easter egg hunting in the garden even when it's not Easter and they play hopscotch out the front. We are still close to the nursery and school. It feels like a country cottage as the sun comes through the kitchen window because the exterior walls face onto two different roads. You have no idea that it's attached to another property at all. There's a sense of history to the house, too. The old irons and fire grates in the cellar and a tin hat from the Second World War; the Victorian ironwork in the garden; the pottery that turns up in the flower beds.

Even Finsbury Park is becoming a little gentrified. There are several fine restaurants and on Blackstock Road a bar that looks like it should be in San Francisco. A pâtisserie has just opened, there's a designer flower shop on Seven Sisters Road along with a new library. Blackstock Road is full of Algerian and Turkish cafés and when Abu Hamza was being filmed outside Finsbury Park Mosque recently on the One O'Clock News, I could see the TV hacks live from my house.

My mum and dad have visited and, after a tour of the three bedrooms, my dad says that I'm a braver man than him because he could never invest all his money in property. He's right, in that interest rates are historically low and there is sure to be another property market crash at some stage. It all feels like the '80s again, with first-time buyers being squeezed out.

The front page of *The Independent* tells me that the average house price in the UK reached just over £150,000 in March 2004. That is about five times the average salary. House prices have doubled in the last five years and are currently rising by 18.5 per cent a year. Britain's current mortgage debt is a staggering £783,000,000,000.

First-time buyers and the low paid are being priced out of the property market not just in the South-east, but all over the UK. The Council of Mortgage Lenders' figures reveal that the number of first-time buyers had slumped to 355,000 in 2003, the lowest figure since records began in 1974.

In March, Bank of England Monetary Policy Committee member Kate Barker warned in a Treasury-sponsored report on housing that the country's obsession with bricks and mortar was unsustainable and was draining dynamism from the economy. In the same month, the Office of Fair Trading discovered that 25 per cent of house buyers and sellers were dissatisfied with their estate agents.

Only what choice do any of us have? We have children who need a permanent home. Nicola wants roots and to see trees grow in her garden and to nurture her own compost bin. We want a home not an investment. If the crash happens, then we can rent out a room or try to sell Nicola's flat again (if the verticality crisis is ever solved). Or I will just have to become a rent boy for real.

You, dear reader, along with my mortgage company, will be reassured to know that every time you buy a copy of this book a small proportion will be going towards paying my mortgage. So place as many bulk orders as you like, tell your friends or, better still, send me large wads of cash.

We have been lucky to get this far. It is only through being a couple and both of us benefiting from inherited wealth that we have managed to buy a house. Without rich parents or inherited wealth then you are, as the mortgage lenders don't quite phrase it, buggered. Even if, way back, I had given up all hopes of freelance writing and become a sub-editor or roving reporter on something like *Staple Manufacturers' Monthly*, home ownership in London would still have been impossible.

Is there any solution? The Mayor of London, Ken Livingstone, plans to force developers to include affordable housing in new projects. Well, it beats playing a tambourine with the Communards. Land belonging to the National Health Service is being sold to build affordable housing, so bad is the crisis.

Other people have suggested building more new homes in New Towns, easing planning regulations, putting more money into housing associations and building more council homes. And at least tax breaks make it easier now to rent a room in your house to a lodger. Perhaps ultimately the market will correct house-price inflation through a long and painful slump and we will be back to the high interest rates and repossessions of the late 1980s.

In Britain, we are obsessed with home ownership. Maybe if we could change our national psyche and be more like other Europeans and find it acceptable to rent, prices would not be driven ever upwards. Or even New York, where the four stars of *Sex and the City* live glamorous lives from rented apartments. The fact that Carrie has blown her house deposit on 400 pairs of shoes is seen as cool rather than incredibly stupid and a direct route to living in Tubeless Clapton.

But changing the national property psyche depends on blaspheming against the spirit of Carol Smillie and Laurence Llewellyn Bowen, and former *Big Brother* winners with big belts for hanging tools on. And also on having decent rented places in which to live where you're not evicted every six months.

Few people in Germany, for example, buy before they're 40. Rented homes are more secure and usually require three-months' notice either way. One friend who's living there tells me there's a whole court dedicated to landlord–tenant disputes, setting rental bands for different types of property and levels for exactly what the rent should be for the floor space in your home. The government insists on 20 per cent deposits before you can buy. Without property inflation there is less incentive to buy to make a quick profit.

Indeed, it's claimed that in Germany there is no such thing as the property ladder.

What I do know is that placing a roof above your head should not be the most difficult thing in your life. My grandfather fought in the trenches in the First World War and my parents were teenagers through the Second World War. The only struggle I've had since I was 18 years old is fighting to get on the property ladder.

It's been a long campaign, fought on many home fronts: Turnpike Lane, West Kensington, Hammersmith, Parsons Green, Fulham Broadway, Camberwell, Neasden, Westbourne Park, Victoria, Elephant and Castle, Highbury and now Finsbury Park. It would be easy to be smug sitting here in my own home having paid the mortgage for a few months. But no, I prefer to paraphrase the words of the great football commentator Bjørge Lillelien when Norway beat England in a 1981 World Cup qualifying match.

LADY PORTER!!! Dame Maggie Thatcher! John Major! Tony Blair! Mr Draper and your withheld deposits! Sloane Rangers! Mr Rachman and your changed locks! Short-life licences! House rotas! Capital Flat-share! *Standard* classifieds! Vase-throwers! Asbestos fibres! Turnpike Lane! West Kensington! Fulham Broadway! Camberwell Green! Neasden Broadway! Westbourne Park! Victoria Street! Elephant and Castle! Highbury Fields! Fitted kitchen manufacturers in New Southgate! Verticality surveys! Abbey National! Bradford & Bingley! Alliance & Leicester! Drivers and Norris estate agents! Hugh Grover Associates (Flats to Buy and Rent in London)! Kinleigh, Folkard & Hayward property services! Davies and Davies! David Phillips! Michael Morris! Hotblack Desiato! Maggie Thatcher! Can you hear me, Maggie Thatcher?! I GAVE YOUR PROPERTY BOYS ONE HELL OF A BEATING!!!

Appendix – LICENCE AGREEMENT

IT IS UNDERSTOOD THAT:

1. This licence constitutes only a permission to use the said premises and confers no tenancy upon the Licensee. Possession of the premises is retained by the landlord subject only to the permission granted in this licence. You are an inferior being and the Daleks are masters of the Earth now.

2. There is no undertaking that rehousing will be provided to the occupants of the premises once the agreement has been terminated and no undertaking to provide former Licensees with cardboard boxes, soup or past-their-use-by-date sandwiches donated by health-food shops.

3. The premises will be returned with vacant possession subject to the conditions laid down in Paragraph 24. Any person found on the premises after the notice has been served will be treated as a combatant and summarily executed without trial.

4. You are an idiot who should have got on the property ladder earlier.

IT IS AGREED THAT:

5. The Licensee will pay the landlord a deposit of one month's rent. The landlord will then place the said deposit in the bank and earn large sums of interest on the agreed sum. The Licensee understands that this deposit is effectively a gift to the landlord as, upon termination of this agreement, she/he will deduct it all apart from the sum of 50p on the grounds that you have not washed the curtains and failed to replace a light bulb in the second bedroom.

6. The Licensee shall not use the premises for any other purpose than as a private dwelling, e.g. brothel, crack den, hypermarket, nuclear-power facility, secret headquarters for employing men in orange overalls who assist you in megalomaniac dreams of world domination.

7. The Licensee shall not do, or permit to be done in the premises or any part thereof, any matter or thing which may be or become a nuisance or annoyance to other occupants of the premises or to neighbouring occupiers. This includes cutting your toenails in the living room and drying your underwear on the bathroom radiator. Noisy sex is not on as the landlord reserves the right to fit paper-thin partition walls throughout the premises. The playing of Queen records at any time is expressly forbidden.

8. This agreement is personal to the Licensee and she/he shall not assign it to any other person; nor shall she/he allow any other person to occupy all or part of the premises; nor shall she/he permit guests – even if they are really fit – to occupy the premises for periods longer than 28 days without the express written consent of the landlord.

9. The Licensee accepts without reservation that the landlord will furnish the premises in as tasteless a manner as possible and model her/his dress sense on Rigsby or Miss Jones from *Rising Damp*.

10. Female licensees and/or occupants of the premises or occupants of neighbouring premises or the female agents of the landlord will complain vociferously and at all times if the loo seat is left up for any period of time on the premises.

11. The Licensee undertakes not to hold any parties, in particular ones that involve vomit down the sofa, cigarette burns on the carpets, bubble bath down the toilet and the theft of sundry meat items from the communal fridge. In the event of such a party, the Licensee undertakes to unconditionally and without prejudice panic and frantically search for the vacuum cleaner.

12. The Licensee shall pay huge energy bills for one-bar electric fires, ancient storage heaters and malodorous Calor gas heaters and agrees to make the necessary arrangements for avoiding hypothermia. Four-season sleeping bags are recommended.

13. The Licensee shall inform the landlord at once should she/he apply for housing benefit and offer material proof that she/he is pressing her/his claim and make the necessary arrangement to have this benefit paid directly to the landlord.

14. The Licensee shall pay full occupancy charges regularly and promptly two weeks in advance. The Licensee shall actively come forward monthly with the licence fees to the landlord or her/his agent and not oblige the landlord or her/his agent to seek her/him out to obtain these licence fees or do any work beyond looking at her/his burgeoning bank balance. Failure to come forward monthly with the licence fees may result in the landlord changing the locks and sending round her/his mate who used to be a nightclub bouncer.

15. The Licensee shall not without the written permission of the landlord:

  • make any alteration or addition to the premises;
  • use a paraffin stove or heater on the premises;

- attempt to get any windows to shut properly or install adequate locks on windows;
- place any picture hooks in the walls of the premises because that would be close to starting to enjoy living in your rented home which is forbidden under the terms of this licence agreement.

16. The Licensee shall be responsible for all fuel bills and undertakes to argue with all other occupants about what is their fair share of the phone bill.

17. The Licensee shall take responsibility for writing down all phone messages for other occupants of the premises on yellow Post-it notes, which then become lost among the mounds of papers and bottles waiting to be recycled.

18. The Licensee shall take responsibility for the upkeep of the garden and maintain the common parts in a clean and tidy condition. She/he will also be responsible for cleaning out the gutters even though this would require a huge ladder and a head for heights which she/he most probably does not have.

19. The Licensee shall take responsibility for bailing out buckets of sewage should the landlord's botched plumbing experience blow-back and flood her/his bathroom with excrement.

20. The Licensee shall not keep any pets, animals or livestock on the premises without permission. The only exceptions granted to this clause by the landlord are a) cockroaches b) rats c) mice d) head lice and e) bed bugs.

21. The Licensee shall supply the landlord with a key to all locked rooms on the premises so that she/he can come in while she/he is out and nose around her/his stuff.

22. The landlord agrees to maintain the premises throughout the duration of this agreement in the condition in which they were

offered at the commencement of this agreement, with furniture from charity shops and skips and her/his brother's off-cuts of flock wallpaper. However, repairs arising from the ill treatment of the premises shall be the responsibility of the Licensee.

23. The landlord reserves the right to terminate this agreement immediately in the case of gross misconduct. Gross misconduct includes: violence or threats of violence against, and racial or sexual harassment of, other occupants of the premises or the neighbouring occupants or agents of the landlord; acts of theft of or deliberate damage to property belonging to or in the safekeeping of other Licensees, neighbouring occupants or the landlord; knowing your rights, voting for the wrong political party, refusing to leave immediately when the landlord or her/his agent seeks to sell the property with vacant permission to a developer.

24. This agreement shall terminate forthwith upon:

- the Licensee ceasing to occupy personally the premises during a period of 28 days;
- the Licensee failing to make any agreed payment within 28 days of this becoming due;
- the Licensee or landlord giving the other 28 days' notice in writing determining the agreement;
- the Licensee failing to wash up;
- the Licensee failing to carry out duties as specified on the house rota;
- the Licensee leaving traces of shaving foam in the sink;
- the Licensee being exposed to asbestos;
- the Licensee having vases thrown through her/his window;
- the Licensee becoming well and truly pissed off with flat-sharing;
- the Licensee by some miracle gaining a foothold on the property ladder.

I accept the offer of this completely worthless licence.

Signed: (Licensee)

Signed: (by or on behalf of the landlord)